Prince or Pauper

*Think Like the Rich
and Beat the System That's Rigged
to Create a Peasant Class*

PETER YACHIMSKI

Prince or Pauper: Think Like the Rich and Beat the System
That's Rigged to Create a Peasant Class

All contents copyright © 2017 by Peter M. Yachimski, RLS. All rights reserved.

Published by More Cowbell Books, LLC.

ISBN-10: 0986053848
ISBN-13: 978-0-9860538-4-9

More Cowbell® is a trademark of Boomvang® Creative Group, LLC, and More Cowbell Books, LLC, respectively. No part of this document may be reproduced or transmitted in any form or by any means (electronic, photocopying, recording, or otherwise) without the prior written permission of the publisher.

Please contact Jake@MoreCowbellBooks.com or write to
More Cowbell Books, 2942 N. 24th St., Suite 114-404, Phoenix, AZ, 85016.

Book design by Jane Gerke

This publication has been compiled based on personal experience, research, and anecdotal evidence, but it is not intended to replace legal, financial, or other professional advice or services. Every reasonable attempt has been made to provide accurate content, and the author and publisher disclaim responsibility for any errors or omissions contained herein. The samples provided are for educational and discussion purposes only. All cited data, websites, publications, and information is from the public domain and was current at the time of publication. Any trademarks, service marks, product names, or named features are assumed to be the property of their respective owners and are used solely for editorial reference, not endorsement. It is the reader's responsibility to tailor the content to his or her own personal or business experience level, goals, values, risk tolerance, and other factors.

Information and insights offered by Peter M. Yachimski, RLS, both herein and through his various investment, consulting, and financial advisory services practices are intended to motivate clients and readers to examine and evaluate current trends, activities, and values for the purpose of recognizing and capitalizing on new opportunities. Any specific recommendations regarding courses of action should be thoroughly assessed in relationship to an individual's overall financial standing prior to making any changes.

CONTENTS

Chapter 1:	The Right Kind of Education	1
Chapter 2:	Learning to Fish	11
Chapter 3:	The Retirement Propaganda	17
Chapter 4:	The New Feudalism	35
Chapter 5:	"I Have This Rich Uncle…"	43
Chapter 6:	One Thing	53
Chapter 7:	Looking through the Curve	61
Chapter 8:	Assets and Liabilities	79
Chapter 9:	The Most Important Word	89
Chapter 10:	Do Your Homework	95
Chapter 11:	The Rule of 72	101
Chapter 12:	Risk vs. Reward	105
Chapter 13:	The Show Must Go On	111
Chapter 14:	Tell Me Who Your Friends Are…	123
Chapter 15:	I'd Rather Be Lucky…	131
Chapter 16:	The Tide Brought Me a Sail	137

CHAPTER 1

The Right Kind of Education

There is a fable from the days of old Arabia, retold by Mark Twain, about a prince who was unsatisfied with his life, despite living in the lap of luxury, and a pauper who longed for the ease that riches offered. Coincidentally, the prince and the pauper were identical twins, separated at birth. Upon discovering each other's existence, they agreed to change places and experience the other's lifestyle—each believing the existence of the other was more desirable. The prince longed for the freedom that came with the release from his station in life, with all of its obligations. The pauper longed for the release from daily labor that wealth afforded.

The moral of the fable is that each one discovered value both in their own lot in life as well as that of their brother. But the underlying lesson that can be gleaned from the fable is that the only real difference between the prince and the pauper—identical twins capable of exchanging places—was the experience and education each had received from his station in life.

The reality is that wealth is both an objective and subjective thing. What some consider to be a meager existence is seen by others as plenty.

In my practice as a licensed retirement advisor and income-planning specialist, I meet with clients from all walks of life. Most are in or near retirement, and virtually all of them have the same problem (or opportunity, depending on your perspective). In fact, we all stand on exactly equal footing when it comes to these two truths:

1. We all have finite resources, whether extensive or meager.
2. We all have a finite amount of time ahead of us, but, with few exceptions, we do not know how much time that is.

Taken together, those truths lead us to ask: Will our resources (savings and investments) last at least as long as the amount of time we have in front of us? Will those resources enable us to live a fulfilling and happy life, or will we be consigned to mere existence, devoid of meaning?

In meeting with hundreds of clients and prospective clients over the years, I have had the opportunity to interview people who have been very successful in their financial preparations, as well as people who have been woefully negligent and/or unsuccessful. As such, here are two more truths:

1. A person's degree of success is in direct proportion to the quality of their financial education.
2. A person's definition of success has a direct and tangible influence on their degree of happiness.

The fable of the Arabian brothers offers frank, though indirect, evidence of the above assertions. A prince would almost certainly be educated to view wealth and its administration differently than a pauper would. Their original station in life might be a result of the education and experience of their parents, but their own experiences and opportunities determine whether they will stay in their inherited station or move to a new reality. (By extension, this also affects their children's initial reality.) Consider, too, that they will have very different measures of success or happiness because of their station, which came both from their inheritance and education. This is what drives them to change, or not change, their station in life. There are many examples of people whose drive pushes them to move upwards on the economic food chain; but it is also possible for those born into wealth and luxury to move down the chain!

Contrary to popular belief, being born into wealth does not guarantee a lifetime of luxury, if the right education is not in play. According to the Williams Group wealth consultancy, 70 percent of wealthy families lose their wealth by the second generation, and an astonishing 90 percent by the third.*

Consider this example from the *Atlantic*, "Where Are They Now? Robber-Baron Edition," Sept. 18, 2015:

Jason "Jay" Gould, the original 19th-century robber baron, is one of the richest American citizens of all time and possibly one of the richest people, ever. He made his money in railroads, by attempting to corner the stock market, and by being what CNBC has called one of the worst CEOs ever… After hiring strikebreakers during a railroad strike in 1886, he was reported to have said, "I can hire one half of the working class to kill the other half."

---

*"70% of Rich Families Lose Their Wealth by the Second Generation," Time, June 17, 2015

Where did his billions go? Jay's oldest son, George, inherited the family fortune. George had seven legitimate and three illegitimate children, all of whom he recognized in his will. But more of George's money went to creditors than to his offspring: He had $30,000,000 to bequeath when he died, according to his obituary in the Times, *down from his father's peak of $77,000,000 (not adjusted for inflation). Yet even that was later revised down by the* Times *to only half as much. After the creditors were paid off, George's children were said to collectively receive a little over $5 million in 1933 dollars.*

An even more recent example is the Stroh Brewery Company, founded in Detroit in the late 1800s. Having survived Prohibition, the company boomed in the years after World War II. A succession of family members leading the company in the 1980s, however, made ill-considered acquisitions, incurred crushing debt, and completely missed the light beer trend. The '90s were no better, and ultimately the brand, once worth in the range of $9 billion, was sold off in pieces. Over the course of six generations, the Stroh family fell from being one of the wealthiest in the country into a mire of personal problems, substance abuse, and tragedies.

Why does it seem so difficult for the success of one generation to be repeated or even built upon by successive generations? Why does the inheritance of enormous wealth and assets so often turn into massive liabilities for the next generation? We'll discuss that more in a moment, but my belief is that far too many people have absolutely no idea what an asset or a liability actually is, what a balance sheet is, what it should look like or how they can change it.

These are lessons that carry into everyday modern life. The disparity in education between the rich and the poor is evident from a recent experience that I had. I wrote chapter 8 of this book while on a flight to visit a client, and happened to sit next to a lovely young woman named Lauren whose job underscores the value that some families place on proper financial education. Lauren is employed as a "Family Education Associate" by a wealth management firm that serves clients with a net worth of at least $25 million. Clients of her firm engage Lauren to visit with their families to provide financial education at all levels and stages of life. When she works with children or grandchildren of the firm's clients—as young as 10 years old—she'll teach how a checking account works, how credit works, how money works, etc. With adolescents, her job is to educate about basic investing and money management—a more detailed version of the "money does not grow on trees" conversation that all parents should have with their children. As a student gets into their 20s or 30s, they are helped to understand how to preserve wealth, tell the difference between bad debt and good debt, understand a balance sheet, and how to protect the family business or its assets. These families hire Lauren's financial advisory firm, in part, because it offers an education that breeds princes—and one that's vastly different from what most Americans receive.

Let's get back to the prince and the pauper. The prince did not value his education. He interpreted the demands placed upon him by his station in life as negative, rather than as a part of his personal growth. He did not want to spend his time consulting with his advisors, looking after his kingdom, and meeting with heads of state and business leaders.

He viewed these tasks as a drain on his life enjoyment rather than necessary work to ensure his future prosperity. He was unhappy, despite being wealthy.

Happiness derives in large part from education, not wealth—an important distinction to make. How many celebrities take their own lives or become addicted to drugs or alcohol because they are unhappy, despite their riches? Conversely, I meet with many people who have modest means but are full of joy every day. Why? Education! Note well that I am not just referring to a structured system of learning, such as college. If you are at a point in life where formal education is not in the cards, do not despair; learning can come from many sources, not just a degree. If you have earned a higher education, I urge you to be open to viewing things differently than you may have been taught—not regarding the basic principles of your profession, but in terms of defining and measuring success. All that glitters is not gold, and all that is gold may not glitter when you sum up the true cost.

Let me tell you a story from my own life that makes that point. My father was a very good provider for our family, with a responsible job at a large corporation that offered good benefits and a handsome salary. His perspective on work and employment, however, was very limited. He had been sold on a vision of retirement—I call it *retirement propaganda*—that includes working one job for one company till a certain age and then quitting cold turkey, because you've earned it. It prevented him from realizing the potential for much greater happiness and wealth than he might have had, both during his working life as well as afterward.

When I was about 17 years old, I was granted an interview with the public works department in the New England town in which I grew up. My father was ecstatic for me over the opportunity. Municipal jobs were hard to come by, and highly sought after according to the common logic of the time. Working for the town meant job security, steady pay, a predictable future, and letting someone else worry about things like health insurance coverage and retirement planning — all very desirable things in my father's view. The interview went well, and I was offered a job riding on the back of a garbage collection truck at a rate of pay of $15 per hour. That may not sound very exciting today, but in 1983, a 17-year-old boy simply did not make that much—and it would have made me quite a success at a young age by my father's standards.

Imagine how upset he was to discover that I had turned down the job offer. Why, he nearly disowned me for my "stupidity"! But, consider this: Had I thrown my lot in with the town, relegating myself to a daily life of collecting garbage in exchange for the then-lofty $15 per hour, do you know how much money I would be making today? About $15 per hour, more or less, adjusted for a few percent per year of inflation. Imagine that: peaking at the age of 17.

Beyond my wages, the benefits package would have entrusted my future to someone else's decisions. What has happened to the coveted municipal golden parachutes? We have seen several municipalities in America file for bankruptcy, in large part due to retirement promises that they did not have the ability to make good on.

Had I followed my dad's guidance, I would have accepted a lifetime of menial labor at an essentially fixed income for life; all for the promise of a secure retirement—only to have that promise evaporate. Instead, I have made a career in real estate and investing. I became a licensed professional land surveyor, a construction finance management consultant, a hospitality development consultant, a licensed financial professional, an investor, a real estate developer, a public speaker, and an author. I am a court-recognized expert in real estate and investments and have been hired as a professional witness on a number of occasions. My clients entrust me with tens of millions of dollars of their money to manage for them. I am an entrepreneur and my time is my own to manage. While I make a very good living, at the top 5% of earners in the U.S. and the top 2% of earners in Arizona, it is even more important to me that my work helps and empowers others by creating jobs and helping communities and individuals become prosperous. I have real meaning in life—which cannot be measured in dollars.

Having a higher purpose than simply making money is extremely important. Donald Trump writes in his book *The Art of the Deal* that he is regularly approached by people seeking a financial investment from him to launch or expand their enterprise. He always asks the question: "What is the purpose of your venture?" If the answer is "to make money," he says that he does not invest, because making money is not a noble-enough cause. If someone's sole purpose is to make money, then when things get tough (as they always will), the venture will fail due to lack of commitment. If the goal has a mission such as bettering the community, creating jobs, preserving history, benefitting the environment, etc., then the person driving the project will have the endurance and passion to weather the inevitable storms. Your personal journey should be the same.

Even if money were not a part of the equation, my life has been much more enjoyable and fulfilling than if I had spent the past 30 years collecting garbage. I am not enticed by the retirement propaganda, because I love getting up in the morning to get to work and cannot imagine a reason why I would ever stop. I pepper fun, recreational activities into my day to keep things lively, and am involved in my community to create a better tomorrow for our children and follow my passions. My life is an absolute joy, and every day is better than the one before.

Is that how you view your life? Would you like to? Then I invite you to read on, because it is there for the taking.

My education has led me to a life that I love, but it was not learning that was offered to me by mainstream society or found behind a school desk. In my opinion, those lessons are intentionally hidden from the population at large, and I believe that debunking the retirement propaganda is critical to your success.

CHAPTER 2

Learning to Fish

I have had the privilege of presenting and speaking to audiences in excess of five thousand people on various topics, as well as serving as a professional expert witness on behalf of clients where millions of dollars were at stake and dependent upon my testimony. In public speaking, there is a simple rule about how presentations are best structured, which goes like this:

1. Tell your audience what you are going to tell them.
2. Tell them.
3. Tell them what you just told them.

That may sound silly or redundant, but it's a time-tested formula for educating people, having them remember the information, and putting it into action.

That is what I am trying to offer to you in this book: an opportunity to change your life in a meaningful and lasting way. I am extremely passionate about this not only because of my own life opportunities and successes, but also because I have been touched (via my family) by the sting of failures due to mainstream commercial, political, and educational systems.

So, let me tell you what I am going to tell you.

In the opening chapter of this book, I noted that my father was an intelligent man who was diligent about preparing for the future—at least in the best way that he knew how. At that time, my career focus was not in the realm of personal finance and retirement planning. I was deeply involved as a professional business growth consultant, assisting business clients with creating expansion plans, business pro formas, getting financing and due diligence in place to secure loans from banks to grow their businesses, etc. My father, although not an engineer by training, was working as the project engineering manager at a large complex in Boston. The year was 1997 and he was 58 years old.

Like most people of his generation, my father had spent a significant chunk of his working life putting money aside in savings, IRAs and 401(k)s. He was looking forward to retirement, only seven years away, and then the unthinkable happened: He was involved in an industrial accident at work that left him unable to continue working. The disability insurance payments, which added up to only a fraction of what he was making in salary, took my mom and dad from enjoying a comfortable lifestyle to living on a strict budget. Mercifully, this situation only lasted a short period of time—when he turned 59½ years old, he was able to start drawing money out of his qualified retirement plans without incurring a 10% early withdrawal penalty. The relief, however, was short-lived, because, what happened in 1999–2000?

The Dow Jones Industrial Average Index plummeted from a high of 11,722.98 on January 14, 2000 to a bottom of 7,286.27 on October 9,

2002. The stock market lost almost 38% of its value, and the retirement hopes and dreams of my father and mother—and countless others—collapsed. I remember very clearly the tremor in my father's voice and the tears in my mother's eyes as they described their situation and asked: "How could our financial advisor let this happen to us? Didn't he know that we can't afford to lose almost half of our money with Dad unable to work? Why would he not protect us and ensure we were not at such a high risk?" They were confused and distraught at the apparent betrayal.

My parents, hard-working and well-meaning Americans, had become paupers. I became determined then to understand what had led them (and most other Americans) down the wrong path to what can only be described as near poverty.

Fast forward to 2008, when the Dow Jones Industrial Average dove from a high of 14,164.53 on October 9, 2007, to a low of 6,547.05 on March 9, 2009—below the bottom of 2002. Called a *correction* by industry analysts, this cataclysmic drop of almost 54% was nothing less than a full-fledged crash. Even those people intelligent enough to try and get out were nearly ruined because you could not sell stocks fast enough to beat the bear. It also meant going against the advice of their so-called financial advisors who were spouting various versions of "Don't panic… the market always comes back…stay in it for the long haul."

The U.S. government and Wall Street have refused to acknowledge that crash of 2008 for what it really was by labeling it a recession. As of 2015, public policy statements claim that our economy has recovered. What's the reality, though? The effects of the 2008 worldwide economic collapse will be felt by many families for decades, if not generations. For perspective, did you know that the stock market crash that ushered in the Great Depression of the 1930s resulted in a drop in the Dow Jones of less than 48%? The 2007–09 crash was far worse at 54%. The futures of many more Americans were destroyed at that time, primarily due to lack of education about how this world and its economic system works.

What I hope to reveal to you in this book is a way of seeing the truth about the economy, the politics, and the education in our country. The goal is to open your eyes to a different way of seeing the world; enable you to recognize real and meaningful opportunity as it presents itself to you; and alert you to propaganda designed to keep you in debt and rob you of freedom during your life.

There are two sides to this coin of education. One is a general perspective, while the other is a series of specific tools to be used in certain situations. By first sharing a general perspective that empowers you to recognize the correct path, I will offer, in this book, a foundation for decision making and of hope. It is important to understand a general perspective before trying to apply any specific information. The reason is simple. You have surely heard the expression, "Give a man a fish and you feed him for a day. Teach him how to fish and you feed him for his lifetime."

Let's say a retirement client wants an answer to a question such as "What is the most efficient way to take money out of an IRA with the least tax consequences before the age of 59½?" For the vast majority of people, becoming a tax-efficiency expert is not a reasonable or realistic prospect. I find a great deal of satisfaction and pleasure in saving my clients a lot of money by providing specific recommendations to resolve that day's challenge. I give them a fish.

However, it is my sincere hope that the information in this book will be enjoyed by countless people who might never have regular access to a private financial consultant. This book is also designed to help protect you against financial consultants who have either been miseducated or are not truly acting in a fiduciary manner—as was the case for my parents during the crash of the early 2000s.

This book is designed to teach you how to fish. I will share information so that you can take charge of your own education and life course. By the end, you will be capable of evaluating a multitude of different situations as they occur during the course of your life, using a few basic, easy-to-remember principles that will shed light on the path most right for you.

Developing the critical eye needed to identify life-changing opportunities—and thereby acquiring the money, assets, and investments that will ensure your family's future—is like learning how to fish. That is the first and most important thing to learn. So, what I am going to tell you in this book is how you can look at life, opportunity, retirement, and our economic and political system differently than you currently may. Doing so will maximize your potential for acting on specific advice from a financial professional.

This reminds me of a conversation with my wife early in our marriage. While she and I started our life together in a humble state of affairs, I was soon earning an ample income from a variety of sources.

That led to a pretty complicated tax return that my wife, a very intelligent woman, struggled to comprehend. She commented that she desired we be careful not to complicate our lives too much that our finances were "beyond her." I responded by stating unequivocally that it was my goal to have streams of income, investments, and business interests that were so complex that we would need a team of CPAs to prepare our tax return. I didn't want to be common, but rather to be dramatically different from most Americans. Today, my CPA employs a multitude of tax-minimizing or tax-avoiding strategies that even I have a hard time following. Goal accomplished!

The lesson in this story is this: Changing your way of looking at money, possessions, assets and liabilities, your budget and even everyday purchases may be intimidating, uncomfortable, and even a little bit unnerving. Don't be concerned with these feelings! Your perspective is what it is because you were taught to think that way—some might call it *brainwashing*, if you are willing to admit that. There is nothing to be ashamed of. Our system is presented as benevolent, but it's actually designed to keep 95% of Americans in the role of pauper.

By the way, with some solid planning, hard work, and reeducation, my parents' situation has since turned out just fine. In fact, they did not suffer at all in the 2008 crash.

Of course, that's not the case for the vast majority of investors and savers, so let's begin the process of learning to fish...

CHAPTER 3

The Retirement Propaganda

What is the education that is offered by our society? In my view, it's a virtual hypnosis sponsored by big business and the government. Here are the steps:

1. Go to college, where you'll select and pay to learn a "career," which you may stay in for the remainder of your working life. You might also keep paying for it for the rest of your life due to student loans—and many analysts believe student debt could be the source of our next economic meltdown.

2. Get a job, ideally with a large company, and keep it as long as you can.

3. Invest your savings, ideally in stocks, and keep them until you die.

4. Entrust your future to someone else. You let your company manage your 401(k), let your broker manage your stock portfolio, let a custodian hold your money in a tax-deferred account, and let the government be largely responsible for your retirement income stream by managing your Social Security account.

All of this adds up to being a lemming: Follow, follow, follow, but don't you dare lead, don't take charge of your own destiny, and don't educate yourself to be responsible for your own future.

By stating the above, I am not espousing anti-government sentiment or anarchy. Both the government and big businesses play a very important role. What I am saying is this: If you want the education that you will need to be successful, happy, and secure in your life, you will need to diligently and aggressively seek it out. It will not be handed to you, and it is not readily available through mainstream institutions. These institutions are designed to create a middle-class mentality, which is really the road of the pauper—although it is presented as something desirable and even lofty.

At this point, you may be asking, "Isn't a large middle class a good thing? Isn't that what makes a society strong and vital?" The answer is no, at least not in the long run, because it is not sustainable. Admittedly, a large middle class works for spurts of short-term economic growth, but history shows us that it will ultimately fail as a societal model. In fact, almost all of the great societies and cultures in history achieved greatness not because of a strong middle class, but because of a tremendous disparity in the economic status between a relatively small rich class and an overwhelmingly large poor class. In other words, there have always been a few princes and many paupers.

Now, history enthusiasts will enjoy the next few pages, but even if you are not a history buff, these stories are imperative for changing your perspective—and they may even challenge what you've been taught through your customary education. It is my goal that the common thread of human experience will plainly demonstrate the need to adjust our perspective and expectations.

Ancient Egypt built its mythical fortune and enduring legacy on the backs of slave labor. (Shortly after the Jews were liberated from slavery, Egypt was overthrown by Assyria as the dominant world power.)

Ancient Greece expanded its empire and wealth with the blood of a conscripted military. (Under Alexander the Great, every male was required to serve seven years in the army.)

Medieval Europe was a lattice of robber barons exacting heavy taxes from the peasant class in exchange for protection within the castle walls.

Medieval Japan was a culture of a handful of shoguns and warlords, with an enormous peasant class shoring up their power. (This continued right up until the 20th century.)

Great Britain colonized the entire world using indentured servitude and slavery as the vehicle for its growth.

In the United States, the economic growth that propelled us into the role of global superpower was driven by policies that enabled the gross exploitation of most of our population. The most notable exception to this pattern is the America of the 1950s and 1960s, which differed for two reasons: 1) the start of the baby boomer generation and 2) the fruition of a new governmental economic policy designed in the 1930s aimed at creating the middle class.

But let's dive a little deeper into U.S. history. After achieving independence, our country was flat broke. The War of 1812 (also fought with Great Britain) nearly collapsed our infant nation. As a society, our first period of great economic prosperity was a direct result of two factors: the sale of federal land to a burgeoning immigrant population and the use of slave labor.

In the early 1800s, America became the world leader in the production and exportation of cotton, controlling a whopping 80% of the world market. This was a function of vast land resources and optimal climate for sure, but it was brutal slave labor that enabled the U.S. to corner the market—as we could produce cotton at lower costs and in larger quantities compared to other nations. Europe experimented with American-style plantation farms, but the social climate of small resident farmers with limited manpower made it virtually impossible to generate the kind of production realized in the American South. Vast empires of plantation lands cultivated by slave labor propelled America to global economic domination. Cotton was one of the most important commodities on the planet. Other nations using slave labor pursued other crops more suited to their geography, such as sugar cane, leaving America virtually unchallenged in worldwide cotton dominance for almost 50 years. The later inventions of the cotton gin and the combine, which mechanized production after the emancipation of the slaves, preserved the U.S. monopoly for a time.

Even after the Emancipation Proclamation, slave labor was functionally replaced with sharecroppers—former slaves renting fields on the plantations from which they'd recently been liberated. Now they were tenant farmers, paying a hefty rent to the same landowners they recently called "master." As a group, their lot in life changed little until the Great Migration of the early 1900s.

Concurrently, in the expanding West, big industry built company towns. These were communities where workers lived in rented housing owned by the company, shopped for food in stores owned by the company, received medical attention from doctors who worked for the company, and so on. In essence, nearly every penny that the company paid out in wages came back to the company in living expenses. Mining boomtowns such as Bisbee, Arizona, are examples of such worker exploitation.

One of the first great industrial endeavors for our country was the development of the railroads, which were built largely by African, Irish, and Chinese workers who lived and died in squalid conditions.

In other words, for the first 125 years of our country's existence, most Americans were paupers.

Then came the Long Depression of the 1870s. This time, and several decades thereafter, was when Vanderbilt, Rockefeller, and Carnegie built their fortunes. These men offered access to commodities that were essential to the future greatness of our nation. They set the stage for the next period of economic growth and assured world economic dominance of the United States for the next 150 years. These princes thought and acted differently than the masses. They were bold, and saw themselves as destined to fill the roles they assumed. Their education was far different from what the population in general received.

Arguably the best investor of our time, Warren Buffett, has often advised to "be greedy when people are fearful and fearful when people are greedy." The men listed above followed a course opposite of the populace, enabling the creation of their economic empires. Doesn't it follow, then, that the majority of people must have been incorrectly educated?

As a rule, when a large portion of the population is doing something, you can almost be assured that it is the wrong thing to do or the wrong time to do it. Take, for example, the real estate boom of 2004–06 in the U.S. As a professional real estate development consultant, I can attest that real estate is one of the most complex, risky, and dangerous investment vehicles there is. Note: I am not referring to buying an extra house and renting it out. I am talking about taking on hundreds of thousands of dollars in debt to 1) acquire land that needs to be subdivided, serviced, permitted, zoned, etc., and prepare it for the marketplace, or 2) buy homes that need major renovations in the hopes that they can be sold quickly, a.k.a., *house flipping*. True, in the arena of real estate investment, enormous gains can be made, doubling or tripling your investment in a matter of months. On the other hand, the numbers of moving pieces, discretionary permits, lender requirements, and local and global economic factors that can cause disaster are almost beyond calculation.

Yet, during this time period, the number of people getting involved in real estate who had absolutely no expertise or experience was mind-boggling. Dentists, auto mechanics, housewives, and every other character you can think of were taking huge risks based on what Wall Street calls *the greater fool theory*. It almost does not matter what you pay for an investment or how much it is really worth, because there is always a greater fool willing to buy it from you at a higher price. We now know that real estate, like any other variable investment vehicle, can and does plummet in value. Millions of Americans' lives were ruined simply because they followed the herd mentality and got into something they knew little about. And thanks to quantitative easing (the introduction of new money into the economy by the Federal Reserve Bank by buying securities like government bonds or mortgage notes, thereby putting cash and liquidity in the economy that did not exist before), our country is now saddled with the burden of servicing billions of dollars' worth of subprime mortgage notes created during that period.

Again, any time there are a lot of people pursuing a certain course, that should give you sufficient reason to pause and critically examine whether there is wisdom in following suit. Like Tommy Lee Jones' character, Agent K, says in the movie *Men in Black*: "A person is smart; people are dumb, panicky, and dangerous!" As a group, people are prone to pursue a dangerous course that they would never even consider as an individual. Keep this in mind.

After the Depression of the 1870s, our population began migrating into the cities, where they were less self-sufficient and were forced to be more dependent upon mass production of food, goods, and services. Rural folks were looking for a better life and opportunities for work. What they got, however, were nearly intolerable and sometimes deadly working conditions in some of the first modern factories. Paid barely a livable wage, men were forced to work twelve- to fourteen-hour days. It was during this time that the first unions were birthed, but in the context of what we are exploring here, it was also during this time of terrible exploitation of the workforce that the United States became positioned to become the dominant military and economic power it remains today.

These terrible working conditions at barely livable wages created the global powerhouse of industrial capacity that eventually led to the wealth of the 1880s through the 1910s. The era was known as the *Gilded Age*, among other things. But up until the First World War (1914–18), the Gilded Age was enjoyed by only a few. The middle class, as we know it today, did not yet exist.

It was this time, and these conditions, that created the environment of miseducation that we still suffer from today. While I am not a professional historian, I believe that understanding this sequence of events is critical. I am not, however, suggesting that the following analysis should be used as a basis for wholesale changes in our government's economic policy. In fact, I will ultimately show you just the opposite. I am trying to explain why our government's economic policies and its educational structure are essential for the economic health of our society as a whole—but are bad for each of us as individuals. Most important, I believe you can take advantage of these conditions to separate yourself from the population at large and ensure your future as a prince.

From the end of the Gilded Age and into the Roaring '20s, it was the lack of a strong middle class that brought the house of cards crashing down. It is for this reason that the education foisted upon us by government and big business today is what it is. Here is what happened:

At the turn of the 20th century, American society was becoming increasingly more urban. People were moving into cities in search of work and modern convenience. The needs of the newly urban society drove innovation, and technology rapidly improved, with new consumer products flooding the shelves of retail outlets. Newly invented factory production processes were churning out these products in anticipation of consumer appetite at a breathtaking rate. The percentage of Americans who had meaningful disposable income, however, was still relatively small—there was no real middle class. The Great Depression of the 1930s happened, in large part, because these factories were borrowing money to produce goods. They had warehouses full of product waiting to be shipped out to retail stores. There came a point, however, when everyone who could afford to purchase these new consumer goods—in the U.S. and around the world—had already done so. The wealthy consumer essentially owned some of everything that there was to buy, so they stopped buying, waiting for the next great gizmo to be invented and put on the shelf. The poor masses could not buy even if they desired to do so, because they lacked disposable income. With the sudden stall in demand, shipments from factory warehouses to retailers came to a screeching halt. With all of that stored product—manufactured on borrowed money, sitting on shelves with no one to buy—manufacturers had no revenue and defaulted on their debts. Their stock values plummeted with their disappearing revenues and their loan defaults. Banks collapsed. Personal fortunes, built on inflated stock values, evaporated overnight. The world was thrown into the Great Depression, which lasted more than a decade.

Some economists will debate my simplification of the events leading up to the Great Depression, but this is not meant to be a college textbook. I am trying to paint a picture for you of some basic socioeconomic conditions that led to the atmosphere we have today.

My wife's recently deceased grandmother lived through the Great Depression. I once asked her to tell me about her experiences, and she explained that her family, and most people that she knew at the time, were almost completely unaware of the existence of the Depression. She grew up on a farm in rural Maine. Her family was essentially self-sufficient. They grew their own food, had livestock for dairy, hunted for meat, cut their own firewood for heat and cooking, and bartered with neighbors to fill in the gaps. They were poor by most standards. While they had plenty to eat and a roof over their heads, they did not have the cash to purchase the newest consumer goods designed to improve quality of life. They were among the large population that either had no need or no money for the newest products being manufactured, leading to the stall in consumer purchasing. So, when the bottom dropped out of the economy, they were essentially unaffected. They were also very happy. They did not miss what they never knew, and the lifestyle they chose was sustainable, despite world economic conditions.

You don't have to listen to CNBC for very long before you'll hear analysts discussing the importance of U.S. companies' efforts to penetrate emerging markets. An emerging market is, loosely speaking, a country or region where blooming urbanization or new availability of technology, jobs, or resources is creating a brand-new middle class. Again, a middle class is defined as a group of people who have achieved a level of income where some portion of their money is disposable, meaning that it can be spent on things that are not absolutely necessary for simple survival. Mind you, many Americans may believe that their cell phones are absolutely required for survival, but that is not really so. We are talking about basic necessities such as food, water, clothing, and shelter from the elements.

We in the U.S. have, in general, an extremely high standard of living compared to most of the world. Almost all of us are already in possession of at least some of, if not most of, the available consumer items we could possibly want. Emerging markets, however, represent a virgin territory for consumer products, because few citizens of these countries already possess those things. These pockets of third-world civilization currently paint a picture of similar conditions to that which preceded the Great Depression! Most people in the developed world already possess the newest available technology; developing countries contain a finite number of people who have disposable income to acquire it; and third-world populations cannot purchase, no matter how much they desire to. Were it not for expansion into countries with current technology infrastructures and an emerging middle class, many American companies would already be experiencing a terrible drop in sales—and stock prices. But even this represents a finite marketplace; eventually something will have to change.

Integral to the economic education that we have been offered by government and business is the notion that we need to live in a city to enjoy modern conveniences and cultural opportunities. The truth of the matter is, though, that big business and governmental services (which are also big businesses) could not exist if there were no metropolitan cities. Census statistics show that more than 90% of our country's population lives on less than 10% of its land area, mostly in about 90 major cities. That means that approximately three hundred million people live on less than one-tenth of our real estate resources. Why?

Think about it: If we lived in a quasi-agricultural society, with only one household every eighth of a mile or so (about one dwelling unit per 10 acres), how could a McDonald's survive? Would you drive 10 miles to get a Big Mac? Of course not! (Well, maybe you would, but that is the subject of a different kind of book.) It takes a much denser population concentration to enable retail outlets to function. In the vernacular of commercial site selection and business planning, we would say that we need a critical mass of rooftops to justify a retail use. Typically, a density of approximately three dwelling units (d.u.) per acre (roughly 120 times as dense as the agro-based community) is desirable to support a 10- or 11-acre plaza, anchored by a grocery store and including a gas station, a few strip-mall businesses, and a fast-food franchise or two. The service area would be about four square miles for a retail center of this size. If you do the math (4 square miles @ 640 acres per square mile x 3 d.u. per acre) that means that about 7,700 households are required to ensure this simple neighborhood retail plaza could survive and thrive. The same population in the rural environment described above would require almost 120 square miles, or a geographic area measuring approximately 11 miles by 11 miles.

Clearly, it is in the interests of big business for our society to live in densely populated cities. Every kind of retailer needs enough people living within close proximity to be even marginally predictable. This is also why we sometimes see business fail: because they have not performed a solid site selection and evaluation process and are too close to a competitor without enough population density to support both operations. Walmart is a great example of the power of good site selection. If you live in a small community, you may wonder why the nearest Walmart is some distance away. The truth is, they will never build one in your area—unless their exhaustive research on population density indicates it will be successful. It is unlikely you will ever see a Walmart fail, not just because they have inexpensive goods, but because they do a thorough job of selecting sites that are sure to be successful based on population. If they decide to come to your community (because demographics support the site selection) it is unlikely that you will be able to stop them.

The same basic principles apply for government and quasi-governmental and municipal entities. In order for a municipality to provide water distribution, garbage collection, and public transportation economically, there must be a critical mass of population density. There can be an argument made that such public services offered to dense population centers are more environmentally friendly than their rural counterparts, but, in my opinion, the jury is still out on that topic. The point is this: There would be no need for massive landfills if our society didn't create enormous amounts of garbage in the form of product packaging, disposable containers, bags, cans, etc. It is all a response to big business driving consumer appetite. My wife's grandmother recalled that family garbage production was almost nonexistent during her childhood. Nothing was wasted and everything was recycled or repurposed over and over again, simply because their rural environment made it too inconvenient to haul away waste.

Similarly, how could an electric utility justify running new power lines at a cost of approximately $400,000 per mile if that line serviced only eight customers per mile? It would take more than 25 years for the electric company to recover their investment before it started to show a profit. Even then, the annual return on investment would be less than 5% per year. That is not a business model that would be well-received on Wall Street or by angel investors. A critical number of rooftops or households is needed to support the infrastructure. Fortunately, particularly for rural citizens, the corporate mentality was quite different in the early 20th century: General Electric, under the leadership of J.P. Morgan, was willing to invest in power distribution infrastructure that would take many years to show a profit. That is rare today.

While the pros and cons of dense communities is the source of ongoing debate, I will make this personal observation. When I was a child, my family of six had a small vegetable garden that covered perhaps a quarter-acre of land. That garden grew so much produce that we froze, canned, jammed, and jellied to preserve for the nongrowing season, and ate like kings all year. Even with all of this provisioning, we had to give away excess and were never wanting. Align this with a study performed by the World Health Organization in 1985, which determined that the available farmable land on the earth, distributed equitably, would provide enough so that every man, woman, and child alive at the time could have two acres apiece—far more than required to provide a bounty of food for the family. In my opinion, there is no reason aside from economics and convenience that requires us to live in densely populated cities, except perhaps that no one really wants to be a small farmer.

This principle applies to virtually every major retail endeavor. You can use this to your advantage if you are an urban dweller. I also know a number of people who live in rural parts of the country, but have business interests in cities and capitalize on that system. My own personal experience is somewhere in the middle. I live in Sedona, Arizona, a small community of about fifteen thousand people and one of the most beautiful places on earth—large enough to justify some nice restaurants and some retail, but small enough to offer a cozy atmosphere in a low-crime environment. From this base of operations, I invest in larger metropolitan areas and travel to oversee development of my investments, consulting for my clients and enjoying culture in nearby cities. Thanks to the Internet, 90% of what I need to do to earn a living can be done from my home office or the office space that I keep in town.

Again, I am not trying to argue that we should live in an agrarian society. I am simply making the point that business and government interests promote the urban environment, which has both positive and negative aspects. It offers conveniences that rural environments cannot, but it also results in social problems that are hard to solve. Just remember this principle: Cities are about control and money. The question is: How can you turn that to your advantage? How can you become a beneficiary of the modern economic model—instead of being a cog in its wheel?

LESSON 1:

If you live in an urban area, as 90% of Americans do, see it for what it really is: a medium to control your expectations, aspirations, spending habits, and even your attitudes about what is valuable and what is not. It is a social hamster wheel that most people do not realize they are on. If you can understand and accept that concept, this will open your mind to a new perspective that will enable you to see opportunities that the majority of people never will.

Take back control of your brain's processing capabilities by rejecting the dogma of big business and government. Empower yourself to make up your own mind. You may choose to live in New York City with eight million other people, or in Big Sky, Montana, with 2,300 other people. Either option is fine, as long as you understand the what and why of it—and how to take advantage of the opportunities presented by the structure of mainstream society and modern technology.

Example:

A doctor friend of mine owns a successful medical practice on the East Coast and recently opened another practice on the West Coast. Both office locations are in urban areas. Additional locations of this dynamic practice are being developed under a franchise expansion plan through other medical professionals so that a multitude of urban areas can be penetrated. The doctor is a true jet-setter, splitting his time between coasts, and loves every minute of it. There is very little about his practices, though, that resembles the modern healthcare system, with its red-tape environment and appalling lack of patient/customer service. Going to the doctor at his offices is more like going to a spa for a relaxing treatment. The spectacular patient experience makes him wildly successful, freeing up much of his time to pursue other interests and do philanthropic work.

CHAPTER 4

The New Feudalism

The prince vs. pauper story line is intended to drive home the importance of seeking out the right kind of educational environment. You need to have the courage to question much of what you may have been taught about money, how it works, and why our country is designed the way it is.

I would like to take this concept of intentional misinformation even further. Indeed, there's a time period in the past that is hauntingly similar to our current economic environment. Understanding the parallel will help you break the chains that are designed to prevent you from realizing your potential.

The feudal period of the Middle Ages—also called the Dark Ages in Europe—lasted from about 500 AD to about 1100 AD. It marks one of the grimmest periods of human history, in part because education was against the law. For the peasant class, learning to read and write was punishable by death. It was during this time that feudal lords built castle strongholds and levied unbearable taxes on the peasant class in exchange for protection. Peasants became tenant farmers, working lands owned by the local baron, duke, earl, or whatever the applicable title was in the region. They paid the vast majority of their crop harvest to their lord for the privilege of running inside the walls of the castle during times of danger. These feudal lords were constantly hungry to expand their lands to increase their wealth. In fact, at the time, the standard measure of a plot of farmland was not based on square feet but on how many bushels of crops could be harvested. An acre of wheat was different in size from an acre of barley. An acre on flat, easily tilled soil was different from an acre of hillside soil full of rocks. The anticipated yield was based on the assumption of one day's work product using a plow drawn by two oxen.

A peasant farmer was assigned an acreage allotment based on the anticipated yield of crops, most of which were paid to the castle in taxes. Do you remember the stories of Robin Hood? If you think he stole from the rich and gave to the poor, you're mistaken. What he was actually doing—if you read the original, non-Hollywood-glamorized stories—was taking back some of the tax assessments and returning it to the farmers from whom it came, so that they would not starve to death. Wealth was not, at the time, measured in money—it was measured in yield potential of land holdings. This can be seen by a book commissioned by William the Conqueror in England in 1086 AD called the *Domesday Book*, which is one of the earliest examples of an assessor's record book—although this document contained no assessor's maps as we have today. The land holdings of William the Conqueror were described in detail, with emphasis placed not only on the size of the properties, but more importantly on the potential yield in foodstuffs. Wealth was defined in terms of food and natural resources, which represented the opposite of poverty. Even hunting for survival on land owned by the local lord or baron was illegal and punishable by death—and, like the prince in our fable, those born into the aristocratic families were educated to see the system in a very different light than the common people. The wealthy class knew that if reading, writing, and arithmetic were taught to the public, they would lose control of the purse strings of society.

One final note about this time period: We must acknowledge that, in most cases, the peasant class was truly in mortal danger without protection. But notice also how the feudal lords used city environments—in the form of castle strongholds—as the medium of control.

Why, though, do I refer to our current economic climate as a "new" feudalism? Because, as recently as 130 years ago, wealth was measured in much the same way as it was 1,500 years ago: in terms of production capacity, largely linked to real estate and natural resources. During the first hundred years of our country's history, the production of cotton, mining, oil, and livestock translated directly into wealth and drove our country into a role as world leader in exports and wealth generation.

Everything changed with the advent of technology. Companies began to manufacture consumer goods, most of which were not related to land management or agriculture. Electricity, the telephone, electric lighting, gasoline-powered vehicles, home appliances—these luxuries became the route to wealth. During the past 50 years in particular, governments have not waged war over real estate; they have waged war over economic superiority. Economic warfare is not just the arena of governments; it is the principle tool of modern business. Think about it: Companies are at war over market share. Stock values are driven by earnings reports, the media, new technology, etc. Big business is no different in its appetite for expansion, disdain for competition, and aggressive practices to subdue its adversaries than any feudal lord.

The other way in which our feudal society differs from the old feudalism is the medium by which the commercial barons extract their tax levy. The 90% of us who live in cities cannot pay these levies in the form of grain or produce or sheep; we have currency at our disposal. We are also more sophisticated in terms of our expectations, so commercial lords have to create a vehicle to get us to give them back our money. Most commonly, this comes in the form of *innovation*.

Prior to World War II, need largely drove innovation. An icebox, for example, meant that a homemaker could keep food for several days rather than making a trip to the market every day. The difference in quality of life for a home that had an icebox over one that did not was immense, and the time freed up by avoiding a daily trip to the market enabled people to be more productive. Therefore, an icebox was developed because people *needed* it. When the market appetite for some invention to satisfy a need was strong enough, someone would go out and innovate to fill that need. In essence, new mousetraps were only invented when the old version of the mousetrap no longer did the job satisfactorily. But the problem with this model is similar to what I discussed in my summation of the Great Depression: At some point, everyone who wanted or who could afford the current mousetrap had acquired one, and so sales flagged. Only when there was a strong need for a new version did one arrive, at which point the market would open back up. Then, in the 1950s, with the advent of television, came advertising.

Suddenly, everyone who already had the current mousetrap readily and willingly subjected themselves to commercials, which convinced them that their current mousetrap, stove, iron, or car was just not good enough anymore. Somehow, these things just did not do the job. Better, faster, longer, stronger, colder, hotter, brighter, or dimmer was not just desired, but absolutely needed. "Keeping up with the Joneses," they called it. Suddenly, instead of need driving innovation, innovation drove need. Instead of a cry for something new preceding the product, companies invented new products or newer versions of existing products and then convinced the public they had to have them. This model is just a form of bullying and really, in my opinion, has robbed American society of the one basic economic principle that made America the freest country on earth: the free market economy.

In a free market economy, the consumer sets the price and the terms. A business can only charge what the consumer is willing to pay. If they push that limit too much, the consumer leaves the marketplace or goes to a competitor. Likewise, the terms of the sale can only be as onerous as the consumer is willing to accept, otherwise they will not consummate the purchase. Let me ask you something: When was the last time that you felt you were 100% in control of the purchasing experience or purchase price?

iPhone 8, anybody?

I recently went to a store to purchase a piece of business software for my new laptop. The clerk handed me a small box, which looked too small to hold a CD to upload the software to my computer. I was assured that everything I needed was there. Sure enough, when I got back to my office, the box contained a card with a registration number on it, which I had to use to access the software download from the Internet. "OK, I can do that," I thought. When I went online to get the program, however, it required a monthly subscription service, which could only be accessed and used while my computer was linked to that company's server over the Internet. Note that there were no markings on the box that told me this was how it would work. I was incensed! How else should I feel about paying hundreds of dollars for a program that I did not even own?

I rushed back to the store and asked to see the manager. I expressed my disappointment with this purchase. If the program did not reside on my hard drive, then how could I accomplish work when not online? What if I was on a plane or riding in a car? What if I took my computer to the beach or on vacation where there was no Internet access? I talked about the injustice of paying for a product that was not actually delivered, and went into a brief tirade about the death of the free market economy.

By now, a crowd had gathered around to listen to my sermon. When I discussed the free market economy and how it was what made America great, and how we as a people had abdicated our birthright by acquiescing to corporate bullying—I received a round of applause from the crowd. People know the difference between right and wrong, and they want to be treated in the way that our constitution imagined. It's no different from the Boston Tea Party. I encourage you to remain steadfast in demanding your birthright to be in control of your destiny. (By the way, I got my money back for that program.)

How else does today's commerce operate within a feudal framework? Here's a quick list:

1. You have been educated to entrust your future to the stewardship of your employer—just as a feudal peasant was coerced to entrust their safety into the castle of his lord.

2. That employer sets your rate of pay and your work schedule, provides for your insurance needs, and sets up and manages your 401(k)—just as a tenant farmer's livelihood and future potential was structured by the lord's land distribution.

3. You're led to believe that security lies in obtaining a job with a large company—just as you could run into a castle's walls in times of distress.

4. Your company constantly seeks ways to capture market share from its competitors, possibly even driving them out of business—just like a feudal lord would lay siege to his neighbor's stronghold to gain control of the land's production potential.

Society has always consisted of a few princes and a vast majority of paupers. Paupers are given or allotted everything they have by the princes, and then they give it back in the form of dependence. If you want to be anything but a pauper, you must seize the appropriate opportunities! Feudal lords took their station of nobility at the tip of a sword; today, you must do it with your sharp intellect. For all its challenges, America remains the Land of Opportunity—just ask any first-generation immigrant.

LESSON 2:

Although opportunity is abundant in the U.S., you still must seek it out. The feudal system is designed to keep you in uneducated servitude. Try not to be co-opted into giving back everything you acquire by being a slave to the newest and best. A wise man once said, "Life does not spring from the things you possess."

CHAPTER 5

"I Have This Rich Uncle..."

At this point, you may be wondering where the roadmap to quick riches is, or why I've spent so much time on history. Rest assured, the background we have covered, and the topics in this and the following chapters, are absolutely necessary to effect meaningful and lasting changes in your life. Without a shift in your educational paradigm and a refocusing of your attitudes toward money, life, and responsibility, even a massive windfall of money would not last. In fact, statistics show that the average person who wins the lottery spends all of the money in about three years—and thereafter finds themselves back in the same boat of bad debt, poor cash-flow management, and living paycheck to paycheck. There are similar statistics regarding people who inherit money from a rich relative.

Without the proper education, no one is equipped to handle sudden wealth and manage it properly so that it lasts and grows. Take professional boxer Mike Tyson as an example. During his career, he earned about $300 million; however, poor education and bad advice regarding his spending habits saw him go broke shortly after he retired.

Sometimes those who managed money well during their own

lifetimes fail to structure their estate properly or educate their heirs—so that shortly after their death, a vast portion of their wealth has evaporated. Take Elvis Presley as an example. When he died in 1977, his estate was worth about $10 million. That may not sound like a lot of money today, but in 1977, $10 million was significant wealth. Sadly, due to poor estate planning, Elvis' heirs only received about $2.8 million. The rest went to legal fees, estate taxes, and court costs.

If you happen to be an individual who actually does have a rich uncle and may be in line for some inheritance, this does not relieve you of the need to improve your education. Without doing so, you may just end up like Mr. Tyson. If you are the rich uncle, then I hope you are as concerned about what will happen to your hard-earned wealth after your demise as you were about its accumulation. Statistically, about 80% of the privately held wealth in this country is in the hands of folks 65 years of age or older, and about 90% of that 80% is held by the top 2% of Americans. Logically, if you happen to be the rich uncle, you probably have a meaningful amount of money to protect and manage.

I often meet with such people in providing financial advisory services, and many have a jaded attitude toward leaving their wealth to their children and grandchildren. I'll often hear comments to the effect of "My kids don't appreciate the value of a dollar" or "My kids would just blow it anyways." To be clear, I am not endorsing living like a stoic so that everything we have goes to our heirs. Enjoy your money to the full while you are alive. But, since few if any of us can predict the exact day we will die, then it is also impossible to create a plan that ensures you spend every penny you have timed exactly to your death. If we are doing proper retirement and income planning, there will most certainly be money left over when we are done with it.

So, I would ask you to consider this: Without proper estate planning, there is an extremely high likelihood that one of three entities will acquire some, most, or all of your money: 1) the IRS, 2) the healthcare system, or 3) the insurance companies. I can tell you with absolute and firm conviction: Each of these three entities has detailed plans and strategies in place to get as much of your money as possible before or after you die. So, whether or not you think your kids or grandkids deserve your leftover money upon your death, ask yourself: Is the government, insurance company, or healthcare system more deserving?

Like any other parent, I have seen times when my daughter isn't making decisions that I believe are well thought out. In fact, at times, my little girl becomes quite frustrating and irritating for me. However, I also know that on her worst day—and I mean her absolutely worst day ever—I love my daughter more than I love the IRS, an insurance company, or a hospital.

If you are the rich uncle or parent—or if, by virtue of the efforts you are making to retool your educational paradigm, you will become the rich uncle, parent, or grandparent—please consider the above exercise. Properly structured, family wealth can change the lives of generations of our progeny.

On the other hand, you may be looking toward a different rich uncle—namely Uncle Sam—to ensure your future. There is nothing wrong with being at least somewhat reliant upon government programs, which have been designed to assist during your retirement years. After all, it is your money, withheld from your paychecks during your lifetime, right? However, please notice that I emphasized the word *assist*. When Social Security was being developed in 1932 and 1933, it was never meant to be someone's primary source of income during retirement. It was meant to supplement their own savings. Furthermore, when Social Security was invented, the average lifespan of an American male was 68 years. There were, at that time, 22 working people paying into the system for every one retired person. Today, that ratio is about three to one.

So, if we are looking to legitimately rely on our Uncle Sam to fund or at least help with our retirement, we really need to understand what his current ability to perform on this expectation is.

Each year at the end of the first quarter, the GAO (the Government Accountability Office) publishes a report detailing the overall financial health of the Social Security, Medicare and Disability fund systems. This fund, the *Old-Age and Survivors Insurance* (OASI) *Trust Fund* is a separate account in the U.S. Treasury, funded by your tax dollars. The trust fund provides automatic spending authority to pay monthly benefits to 1) retired-worker (old-age) beneficiaries, 2) their spouses and children, 3) survivors of deceased insured workers, and to 4) disabled workers. With such spending authority, the Social Security Administration does not need to periodically request money from Congress to pay benefits.

Funds not withdrawn for current expenses (benefits) are invested in interest-bearing federal securities, as required by law, and the interest earned is also deposited in the trust fund. The OASDI, originally created under and in response to Social Security Act Amendments of 1939, also established a Board of Trustees. OASI became effective on January 1, 1940, and superseded the old-age reserve account established under the Social Security Act of 1935. These monies are what Uncle Sam has earmarked to help fund your retirement.

The 2014 OASDI Trustees Report—officially called *The 2014 Annual Report of the Board of Trustees of the Federal Old-Age and Survivors Insurance and Federal Disability Insurance Trust Funds*—presents the current and projected financial status of the trust funds. The 2014 report is for the 2013 fund year activity.

A couple of notes: I have italicized, and in some cases underlined, the most pertinent information, and inserted my comments in parentheses. The actual summary is far lengthier and more confusing than the excerpts I have selected here. I have cut out pages of long-winded rhetoric and five-dollar words to help you focus on the real importance of the summary report—which is downright frightening. I encourage you to read the entire report, which is available online at www.ssa.gov. Ready? Here we go....

Section 2A (Overview and Highlights):

At the end of 2013, the OASDI program was providing benefit payments to about 58 million people (Author's note: This is about one out of six Americans): forty-one million retired workers and dependents of retired workers, six million survivors of deceased workers, and eleven million disabled workers and dependents of disabled workers. During the year, an estimated 163 million people had earnings covered by Social Security and paid payroll taxes. <u>Total expenditures in 2013 were $823 billion.</u> Total income was $855 billion, <u>which consisted of $752 billion in non-interest income.</u> (Author's note: Meaning they collected less money in direct revenues than they spent in benefits) and $103 billion in interest earnings...

Short-Range Results:
Social Security's cost exceeded its tax income in 2013, and also exceeded its non-interest income, <u>as it has since 2010.</u> This relationship is projected to continue throughout the short-range period (2014 through 2023) and beyond. The 2013 deficit of tax income relative to cost was $76 billion and the deficit of non-interest income relative to cost was $71 billion...*For 2014, the deficit of tax income (and non-interest income) is projected to be approximately $80 billion....*

The projected reserves of the DI Trust Fund decline steadily from 62 percent of annual cost at the beginning of 2014 until the trust fund reserves are depleted in the fourth quarter of 2016. At the time reserves are depleted, continuing income to the DI Trust Fund would be sufficient to pay 81 percent of scheduled DI benefits. The DI Trust Fund does not satisfy the short-range test of financial adequacy....

Beginning in 2020, annual cost exceeds total income, and

therefore the combined reserves begin to decline, reaching $2,698 billion at the end of 2023.

Long-Range Results:

The Trustees project that annual OASDI cost will exceed non-interest income throughout the long-range period (2014 through 2088) under the intermediate assumptions. The dollar level of *the theoretical combined trust fund reserves declines beginning in 2020 until reserves become depleted in 2033. Considered separately, the DI Trust Fund reserves become depleted in 2016 and the OASI Trust Fund reserves become depleted in 2034. The projected reserve depletion years were 2033 for OASDI, 2016 for DI, and 2035 for OASI in last year's report...*

The retirement of the baby-boom generation will increase the number of beneficiaries much faster than the number of workers increases...

Conclusion:

Under the intermediate assumptions, the Trustees project that annual cost for the OASDI program will exceed non-interest income in 2014 and remain higher throughout the remainder of the long-range period...and become depleted and unable to pay scheduled benefits in full on a timely basis in 2033...

For the combined OASI and DI Trust Funds to remain solvent throughout the 75-year projection period: (1) revenues would have to *increase by an amount equivalent to an immediate and permanent payroll tax rate increase* of 2.83 percentage points (from its current level of 12.40 percent to 15.23 percent; a relative increase of 22.8 percent); (2) *scheduled benefits during the period would have to be reduced by an amount equivalent to an immediate and permanent reduction of 17.4 percent applied to all current and future beneficiaries*, or 20.8 percent if the reductions were applied only to those who become initially eligible for benefits in 2014 or later; *or (3) some combination of these approaches* would have to be adopted.*

These last few sentences are extremely important to grasp and digest. What the government is saying here, in short, is that the Social Security and Disability benefits systems are going to run out of money unless current and future benefits are reduced, taxes are increased, or both.

It is clear that the government, and likely many other institutions, will not be able to keep the promises they have made. That is why the most important word for our era is *math*. Once they realize what's happening, many people become outraged and cry for a change in leadership. Democrats blame Republicans for mismanagement of the government and taxation policy. Republicans blame Democrats for expensive entitlement programs. We all want to believe that if we could just change our leadership, it would fix everything.

---

*SOURCE: https://www.socialsecurity.gov/OACT/TR/2014/II_A_highlights.html#76460

The reality is, however, it is just math—and math has no politics. Math treats everyone exactly the same. No one can escape the simple math of social demographics or inflation. The math will catch up to you, no matter how fast you run. What you have to do is embrace the truth behind this math and make it work for you, rather than against you.

Can that be done? Absolutely! Do we have proof of that? Yes, we do! As we've discussed, Vanderbilt, Carnegie, Rockefeller, J.P. Morgan, and others built vast fortunes during the Depression of the 1870s. Henry Ford built an automotive empire through the Great Depression of the 1930s. Most of the public utility companies were built during the 1930s. Incredible empires grew out of the most challenging times—and paupers became princes. Do you think that this transformation happened to people who got lucky…or to people who educated themselves in a different way than the masses and took control of their destinies?

The answer is clear. The good news is that you are opening your mind to see things as they really are—not as you wish they were—and that is a very important first step on the road to escaping the trappings of the new feudalism. Once you get comfortable with that, once you get comfortable with the math and not terrified by it, then you can begin to remake your paradigm based in reality rather than fantasy.

LESSON 3:

No one can fix things for you but you. That is a good thing—because only you understand what your hopes and dreams are and what you value in life. Only you can map out a way to get there that is really in your best interests. To leave such important work to someone else is to court poverty and slavery, and you are neither a slave nor a pauper.

You are free. You are no longer a lemming racing toward the edge of a cliff with the rest of society. Taste the free air that is self-determination. You now have the whole world opened up to you. Where will you go from here?

CHAPTER 6

One Thing

In 1991, Billy Crystal and Jack Palance starred in a buddy film called *City Slickers*, which was rich with lessons about second chances, friendship, and manopause. In my view, the most poignant and important of the many messages centered on a scene where Mitch (Crystal's character, the city slicker) and Curly (Palance's character, the trail boss) are chatting while following some cattle on horseback. Curly expresses the simplicity of cowboy logic about love and life, and Mitch responds, "That's great— your life makes sense to you."

Curly replies with mild disgust, saying, "You city folk worry about a lot. You spend about 50 weeks a year getting knots in your rope and then you think two weeks here will untie them for you. None of you get it. Do you know what the secret of life is?" He holds up his index finger. "Just one thing."

"What's the one thing?" asks Mitch.

Curly responds with the seven words that have resonated with me ever since: "That's what you have to figure out." No, he was not being a smart aleck. He was giving incredibly sage advice we should all heed.

The concepts discussed in these pages, once successfully absorbed, can free you of mental and financial slavery. Success and wealth must be defined in ways that are not controlled by mainstream propaganda. You must shed the burden of all of the intentional miseducation and begin the process of self-determination. Your mind is free, but there is also a void: You now have a problem to contend with. You may have spent your entire life, whether that is a long time or a short time, pursuing goals laid before you by the dogma. In the baby-boomer world, the ultimate lifestyle expectation was a four- or five-bedroom house in suburbia with a white picket fence, a three-car garage, and a job with a pension, allowing a modest but comfortable and predictable retirement by age 65 on a fixed income provided by a pension and Social Security. A few of the baby boomer generation have successfully reached that goal—although far fewer than set out to do so.

Based on the overall results, it's reasonable to question the validity and the sanctity of that path. Once you do, you may not be sure that a fixed-income retirement is either achievable or even desirable. It is up to you to fill this void with your own vision of the future. To get there, you will have to chart a course, develop a plan, set priorities, and start making choices. In other words, you will need to figure out what your one thing is. You need to make it work for you, and be faithful to it.

So, what does that process look like? Let me give you an example.

When my daughter was 18, she had set a goal to travel to a third-world country to do some missionary work. It was all she talked about and all she worked toward. Now, you may think that such a philanthropic obsession would easily drive all of her decisions, but one day she came to me with a problem of sorts. She was considering buying a new car to replace her old-but-reliable one. She was in college at the time and so had limited resources. She wanted my advice on buying a car on credit: how to negotiate the deal, what were reasonable terms, was it better to have an affordable payment or save money on interest and struggle with a larger payment, etc. All I had to do was to ask her what her one thing was. "Well, my trip to South America, of course," she said.

So I asked her, "What would happen if your travel visa came through, the invitation was extended by the missionary group, and you had just one week to make preparations and be at the airport—but now you're responsible for an auto loan?"

She immediately saw that the decision wasn't about financing, affordability, or make and model. It was simply: How would buying a car potentially impact, or even endanger, her one thing? Making the decision in that light was very easy. She continued to drive the older car, and, when the door was opened to her one thing, she stepped through without any entanglements. She enjoyed a five-month visit to Guyana that changed her life forever. I was so proud of her.

She found success and happiness because she freed her mind from the manipulation of consumer advertising and the peer pressure to keep up a certain appearance. A new car might have made her feel good for a short time while she sat behind the wheel and it was still bright and shiny. But eventually, the car would deteriorate and she would be forced to get another new car to maintain the high—trapped in a self-perpetuating cycle of self-esteem based on the vision of success imposed upon her by commercial dogma rather than actual value. Like so many others, she would have been fooled by society's mistaken belief that liabilities are assets.

A car (or anything else that depreciates in value but requires a static or increasing cash outlay) is a liability, not an asset. A liability takes, while an asset gives. In my daughter's case, a new car would depreciate in value and would demand more and more in the form of steady payments, increasing repair bills, insurance, gas, time to maintain, etc. What's worse, the effects are cumulative, because many people purchase a car on a loan that outlives the vehicle; i.e., the next purchase must finance not only the next car, but also any residual debt from the current car that cannot be retired with its trade-in value. It becomes a vicious cycle that, over a lifetime, can devour enormous amounts of your wealth, security, and happiness. The only time that a car is an asset is: 1) when it is a business vehicle that you use to make deliveries or drive to conduct business, the cost of its use is built into your pricing with a profit margin, or if you can charge a client for mileage at a rate higher than the average mileage cost of use, or 2) when it is a limited-edition collectible that actually increases in value due to demand—and then only when there is a strong and reliable resale market. A collectible has no intrinsic value when there is no reasonable hope of reselling it.

Take art, as an example. The March 15, 2012 issue of *The Bottom Line/Personal* publication quoted Terry Kovel, an authority on valuing collectibles, in the article "10 collectibles not worth collecting anymore." Kovel identified a number of items once thought to be collectible art and explains how many collectors were duped:

> Thomas Kinkade paintings and prints were produced in such huge quantities that they now have very limited resale value. If you paid retail prices for these paintings at a Thomas Kinkade Signature Gallery—there were more than 300 such galleries in the 1990s—you almost certainly will never recover most of the hundreds or thousands of dollars you paid. Scores of Kinkades are available on eBay, and most receive no bids.

My mother-in-law has collected a number of Hummel figurines, and her mother collected Franklin Mint plates. Both were convinced they represented investments and their collectible value would increase—but both of these items are also, unfortunately, on Kovel's list. It's not that I am trying to expose the investment mistakes of my loved ones, it is that I am trying to paint a picture for you of what actually has value: An asset is only an asset if you can actually sell it and convert it to cash, at will, for a profit.

Now, some of you, defending your new car purchase, are saying right now, "Hey, if my new BMW that I struggle to afford makes me feel good about myself, then there is value in that which equals or exceeds the cost. That makes it an asset of intangible value." Is that true? The answer is a resounding "Hell no!" If the car truly makes you feel good about yourself, you are caught in an infinite loop of chasing self-esteem based on the values imposed upon you by the commercial system. The only way for you to maintain that self-esteem is to constantly be purchasing new vehicles. You are addicted to a drug that will keep taking and taking from you for your entire life as you pursue the next fix. That makes it the worst kind of liability.

Am I saying that no one should ever buy a new car? Of course not! I am simply saying, "See it for what it really is: a liability." Make a decision to minimize that liability, so that the greatest possible amounts of your resources are available to accumulate assets. Can a car make you feel good? Sure it can. But, to quote another film—about the Jamaican bobsled team's Winter Olympic aspirations—called *Cool Runnings*: "If you are not enough without it, then you will never be enough with it." Self-esteem does not come from the things we possess, whether they be material goods, trophies, or adulation from others; it comes from within.

My daughter is an example we can all relate to at some level. She did not buy the new car, and therefore avoided the shackles that could have prevented her from taking her missionary trip. Instead, she went to Guyana and had an experience that shaped her thinking, values, self-worth, and self-esteem. It affected how she measures success and happiness, has improved the quality of her marriage by helping her maintain focus on what is really important in life, her attitude toward work, her generous spirit, and her psychological rewards center. Yes, the trip required five months of her time and cost several thousand dollars, but the experience—unlike a new car—will give back to her for the rest of her life. That is an asset of both intangible and incalculable value, including the fact that it improved her decision-making abilities.

LESSON 4:

What is the secret of life? Just one thing. What is it? That's what you have to figure out.

CHAPTER 7

Looking through the Curve

> "I am not a product of my circumstances,
> I am a product of my decisions."
>
> —*Stephen R. Covey, author of* The 7 Habits of Highly Effective People

> "The moment you take responsibility for everything in your life is the moment you can change anything in your life."
>
> —*Hal Elrod, author of* The Miracle Morning: The Not-So-Obvious Secret Guaranteed to Transform Your Life (Before 8AM)

Having identified your *one thing*, this object of your desire now rightly becomes the object of your pursuit. Whether it's riches, travel, retirement to a tropical island, or philanthropy, the universe will not simply drop results into your lap. You must manifest your desire by taking decisive actions to make it a reality—and reject any tendencies toward making excuses for not achieving your goals.

Some may say, "I know exactly what I want out of life," and yet I know many who go through life frustrated and resentful. They always have stories of how some endeavor did not turn out well, how some effort did not pay off, or how the world has not been cooperative with their journey toward wealth. Their lot in life is a result of the world conspiring against them. They are victims.

I won't make a blanket statement, such as "You get out of it what you put into it" or the like, which suggests that all of the fault lies with the individual making the complaint. Certainly, we're all susceptible to the occasional misfortune, and sometimes the conditions around us simply do not seem to offer up opportunity. The Great Recession of 2008–12 taught us that. Many well-educated, hard-working people simply could not find gainful employment no matter what they did. I personally experienced the pain of being without opportunity or liquidity for an extended period of time, which was painful and at times demoralizing. Even in my darkest hours, though, there were certain principles that I held dear and practiced that set me up to win. No matter how difficult times became, I often said to my daughter, "Whether you have a good day or a bad day is a decision that you make the moment you open your eyes in the morning." Winning is not a matter of the right circumstances; it is a matter of visualization and making small, daily decisions that inexorably move you toward your one thing. With this attitude, when opportunity ultimately did present itself, win I did. That is what I want to discuss now: How to set yourself up to win. How to use the tools, mindset, and atmosphere to ensure the greatest possible success as soon as the opportunity knocks on your door.

Thomas Edison famously said, "People miss opportunity because it is dressed in overalls and looks like hard work." The reality is that many Americans have been sold a lie that wealth, fame, and power will just fall into their laps one day. Nothing could be further from the truth.

Opportunity for wealth is cultivated like a garden over a period of time, often through hard work, sacrifice, and relentless belief in one's self and faith in the inevitability of one's own future success. As Robert Herjavec of *Shark Tank* once said, "It takes 10-15 years to become an overnight success." The truth and importance of that statement is proven over and over again by truly successful people and companies.

The good news is that in America, like no other place on earth, you can in fact realize success and wealth by the value of your own hard work and by the power of your faith. But these few words of encouragement are not enough, are they? What we really need to talk about is how you can stack the deck in your favor, so that you can capitalize on opportunities and reach your dreams as soon as possible. This is done through visualization and manifestation. There have been many, many books written about the importance of visualization, but it can be an elusive skill to develop. I want to tell you how I finally became able to define this valuable trait, which I have used all of my life instinctively. This gift came to me through one of my passions—motorcycle racing—and by practicing the principles discussed in chapter 15, creating your own luck.

Now, I think it is important to frame this life-changing event with a few details. Up until 2012, at the age of 46, I had never ridden a motorcycle. The sport of motorcycle racing is extremely physically demanding; like most other physically demanding sports, the most competitive participants begin in their early teen years and peak in their twenties or thirties. The commitment it takes to be a winner in motorcycle racing is extremely high in terms of time, training, and money. Because I started racing when I was 49 years old, I had a lot of ground to cover to achieve my goal, which was to simply become competitive within my first year. By applying the same principles that drive every opportunity that will ever present itself to me or to you, I was able to not just meet, but exceed my goal.

Using the following principles in combination with each other magnifies their power and will create in you an unstoppable force for change and success.

Let's start with the principle of *visualization*, discussed at length in Napoleon Hill's legendary *Think and Grow Rich*. Hill contended that, to be successful in the pursuit of wealth, you must be able to visualize yourself holding the money in your hands and affirmatively deciding on a specific date at which time the money will appear. He cites several examples of people who have done just that and succeeded.

A modern-day example is actor Jim Carrey. In a 1997 interview with Oprah Winfrey, Carrey told how, at one point, his entire family lived in a camper van on a relative's lawn. When he arrived in Hollywood at age 19, Carrey found that success was elusive. In 1985, a broke and depressed Carrey drove to a spot overlooking Los Angeles and he wrote himself a check for $10 million for "acting services rendered," post-dated it 10 years, and kept it in his wallet. He made his $10 million in 1994 on the movie *Dumb and Dumber*—one year ahead of schedule. But what does visualization involve? Many of us have a mental block against it, because our minds are not trained by the educational system to operate this way. Mainstream education trains us to not visualize the goal, but to pick apart the process of getting there and break it down into component parts. Think about how you learned to solve for "X" in mathematical equations. You had to learn the rules of taking each individual step in the process, breaking down the process, and writing it all out. You were graded not just on whether your answer was right or wrong, but also for showing your work and whether or not you had the steps detailed and in the correct order.

While this process of breaking down problems into pieces is often necessary, it fails to acknowledge the power of the subconscious mind. Mainstream education focuses on the conscious: surroundings, circumstances, laws, and conditions. More often than not, however, success occurs in the gray area of the instinctive and subconscious, which is harder to explain. Learning to access this through visualization is vital in mapping the road to your one thing.

As a newcomer to the sport of motorcycle racing, I had not developed the muscle memory and instinctive responses that I'd have had if I started in my teens. The first thing that I did, therefore, was to enroll in an advanced (not beginner's) riding clinic. Although I was a novice, I was not interested in being an amateur rider. I wanted to be a motorcycle racer. The clinic was called Total Control, and in addition to the physics and mechanics of how a motorcycle operates, and techniques for maximizing control, speed, and safety, it included psychological conditioning to aid in controlling fear and maintaining focus.

This was the exercise in visualization:

The instructor placed a bottle of water on the floor five feet in front of me and told me to close my eyes, walk to the bottle, and pick it up. At that distance, success came easily. Then, the water bottle was moved to 10 feet away. Again, I closed my eyes, walked over, and picked it up.

Each person in the class took turns at increasing distances. At 20 feet away, most of us were not able to pick up the water bottle on the first attempt; after one or two failures, many succeeded, because each attempt enabled us to make adjustments. But that was about approaching the problem with the conscious mind, breaking it down, counting the steps, measuring our pace, etc.—not the subconscious, which is far more powerful. There's nothing wrong with learning from your mistakes, but it's a flaw to think that's how the real world always works. For most people, the opportunity to become a prince doesn't endlessly repeat itself in the same manner during the course of your life so that you can eventually get it right.

This is why and how visualization in your subconscious becomes paramount for success.

When my turn came at 50 feet, I missed several times—it was impossible to make adjustments for all of the variables with my eyes closed. Counting steps did no good if they varied by half an inch from my previous try. Fatigue affected my equilibrium, so staying in a straight line was nearly impossible. Covering the distance at exactly the same speed over and over again could not be done precisely enough.

After several attempts, it became clear that using my conscious mind to attack the challenge was a losing proposition, especially when you added the mounting frustration and laughter of my classmates. At that point, I finally absorbed the lesson that was being taught: As with so many things in life, I simply could not consciously manage all of the variables that drove the outcome. I had to release control and simply visualize the goal.

I cleared my mind of all of the calculations, past experiences, and failed attempts, and blanked out the noise around me. I saw, in my mind, the water bottle. Not on the floor in the middle of a room full of people, but just the water bottle in a white space. I visualized the prize, without any distractions, acknowledgement of the difficulty, excuses for prior failure, information, or thought of what it would take to get there from here. Bottle. Plain white background. There was not even a hint of doubt that the bottle would be in my hand in a few moments. That bottle belonged to me and I was going to get it. I closed my eyes, walked the 50 feet right over to it, bent over, and picked up the bottle.

In the moment after I picked up the bottle, I was not even surprised at my success. Of course I had the bottle in my hand. It was mine, after all! Then, the truth of my experience hit me: The visualization of the goal is not about making a plan for how to accomplish the goal. It is about owning the goal and going over and getting it, because it belongs to you—just as your future as a prince belongs to you. It is only your own mind, your own consciousness, your own insecurities, and your own self-imposed limitations that prevent you from going over and picking it up. When you visualize yourself as a prince, whatever your vision may look like, you must not get hung up in the how and when and where and why and if. You must visualize your success in your subconscious as if it has already happened—as if you are already in possession of the coveted goal. Once you are a prince in your subconscious mind, then you will start acting like a prince, thinking like a prince, and walking confidently toward the goal like a prince, because it belongs to you. You are, in fact, already there in your mind and heart.

It was an interesting experiment, and I recommend you try it yourself to see if you can repeat my experience. But it's important to note the practical application, too, so let me take you out to the racetrack.

A motorcycle track includes many curves, some tight and some more modest. There is a practice in racing called *looking through the curve*, which is an application of the visualization principle. When you enter a curve, you do not look at the track 10 or even 30 feet in front of you. At velocities in excess of 100 miles an hour, that's just not enough distance to avoid other riders, adjust speed, increase or decrease lean angle, or make the many other tiny adjustments to keep from crashing. Instead, you turn your head to look at the very end of the curve. As you lean into the curve, your body, your ears, and your peripheral vision all communicate information, which your mind is processing in the background to get you to the end goal—in this case, exiting the curve safely and at the highest possible speed into the straightaway. You are not consciously aware of all of the adjustments; they just happen to enable and facilitate your goal. It is a magical and beautiful experience. More experienced riders even look beyond the end of the curve. If there's a series of curves that proceed generally in the same direction, the fastest rider is looking out beyond the limits of the track at a power pole or a smoke stack in the far distance. They head for that marker, while their body and machine navigate the curves right and left in the periphery—not in the conscious mind. In their minds, they are already there at the end, just as the bottle was already in my hand before I took the first step. What happens along the way to get there is a side point.

Visualization on the racetrack is the difference between winning, going slowly, or in a worst case, crashing. In your journey toward becoming a prince, visualizing yourself already there is the key to automatically taking the necessary steps along the way. Once you have that firmly seated in your mind, all other things become as natural and automatic as breathing.

One word of caution on visualization: The same principles that will lead inevitably to your success can also, if not managed, lead just as easily to failure. On the track, it's known as *target fixation*, which happens when you see an obstacle in front of you and become so focused on it that you cannot avoid it. A racer might round a corner and see another rider crashed on the track in front of him. In this event, a racer must spend only enough time and attention on the crash to acknowledge it, enabling the body to subconsciously adjust and avoid it. If the rider looks too long at the crash—fractions of a second—the mind will fixate on the calamity and the body will steer right into it. It becomes unavoidable.

The same thing can happen in the journey of becoming a prince.

Rounding a corner, you'll see that someone else has crashed. You will see their life in a mangled heap and their anguish over the temporary setback. You must be very careful not to become fixated on the potential for calamity. Fixation equals paralysis. Even if you decide to stop and help (a dangerous thing to do on a race track, so let's assume another circumstance), paralysis could prevent you from acting decisively to save a life. In your race, though, dwelling too long on failure will divert you from your victorious course, leaving you emotionally and psychologically unable to achieve your own goals.

The second principle is to *surround yourself with success*. You need people and resources who will elevate you quickly.

When I started motorcycle racing, I set a goal to be competitive within my first year in the sport, but I had none of the tools available to become competitive quickly and efficiently. A good friend of mine introduced me to a racing team that had everything that I needed and was willing to shepherd me along. This did not come cheap, in terms of time or money, since I made numerous trips across the country to train and practice—but I knew that's what was required to set myself up to win.

Here are the tools and resources that helped get me where I wanted to go:

Equipment: The team supplied the motorcycles, all in peak mechanical performance condition. I did not need to learn what goes into a high-quality machine or waste time seeking it out.

Support: The team provided skilled mechanics for each training, practice, and race event. I didn't need to get my hands dirty doing repairs, nor did I worry that the tuning of the motorcycle wasn't perfect.

Supplies: The team provided the racing fuel (not ordinary gasoline), the tires (several kinds for different conditions), the food, the refreshments, even a place to take a nap between races. Without those concerns, my machine and body were always capable of optimal performance.

Coaching: The team provided a coach who watched me on the track, watched video of my practice sessions, talked me through the more technically challenging aspects of each race venue, and helped me prepare emotionally and psychologically for each event. He showed me the best lines around the track for the most efficient course, and how to enter and exit each curve correctly for the highest possible level of safety and speed. He gave me counsel, commendation, and encouragement so that my performance curve was as rapid as possible.

At the risk of oversimplifying, all I had to do was show up, suit up, and get on the bike, and I was well on my way to my goal of being competitive within the year. The approach I took enabled just that.

But there's more. Racing down straightaways at speeds of 150-plus miles per hour and going through curves as fast as 100 miles per hour, I needed to control my fear of injury or even death. Using the tools and resources described above enabled me to focus on my performance in the following ways:

With my equipment in peak condition, I did not need to fear that a mechanical problem might result in a crash, or that my equipment was unsuitable for the task.

The support I received, both mechanical and coaching, eliminated the fear that equipment would fail at a critical moment. I knew the tires were just right—tread, wear, hardness, air pressure—for the conditions on any particular day, and the tuning of the suspension was appropriate for the pavement surface. I didn't need to be concerned that a choice I might make in ignorance could be potentially fatal.

Since the team provided supplies, I did not need to fear whether the gasoline was optimal for best speed. I could turn my attention and brainpower to mental preparation, proper hydration and nutrition, and relaxing and recharging between races to manage fatigue.

Finally, expert coaching removed the fear of my own ignorance and inexperience.

All of these things, put together, helped me to completely shed any fear. In my first race, I notched a third place and a first place in a series of seven races. (OK, the first place came in a race of my own age group. It's not like I was racing against 17-year-olds, but give a middle-aged guy a break.) I had set out to become competitive, and my trophy plaques are proudly displayed in my office to remind myself of the principles described above.

Even if you never set foot on a racetrack, these same principles apply to your life and business. You must surround yourself with the best available people and resources that you can afford. My business team includes outstanding CPAs, architects, engineers, attorneys, and bankers—not to mention mentors, consultants, and support staff. If I need an answer to a question, I can pick up the phone and get expert information quickly and efficiently. That way, I can focus on making decisions and moving toward my goal, not on the mundane tasks that yield little return on investment for my time. Just like my racing team, these trusted advisors enable me to move forward without fear of failure, which means I can execute much more confidently and quickly than my competitors.

A word of caution: Just as surrounding yourself with expert people and resources can enhance your efforts exponentially, tolerating anything less than excellence can cripple you beyond recovery. If you have an employee who wastes time or product, displays a negative attitude, or treats your customers without reverence, you must act decisively. They are stealing from you and your family, and must be cut loose to enable your success and happiness. If you have an accountant, doctor, mechanic, electrician, or other service provider in your personal or business life whose performance is less than excellent, you need to trade up. If you have friends who are critical, demeaning, or unsupportive in any way, you need to excise them from your life. They may not be bad people, but experience shows that if anyone tells you that you can't accomplish something, they are only projecting their own fears and insecurities onto you. Do not tolerate anything less than excellence in your life from yourself or those around you, and life will pay you back handsome dividends.

Any racer will tell you that the winner is not the one who enters the curve fastest, it is the one who exits the curve fastest. It takes little skill to ride a motorcycle down a straightaway with the throttle wide open. Anyone can go fast in a straight line. The danger, and the area where the highest level of skill is required, lies in the curves. I can testify firsthand that if you approach a curve too fast, you can run right off the track.

If you lean into a curve too soon or too late, you risk losing speed or colliding with another rider. Because it takes time to gain momentum, exiting the curve correctly sets your line for the next curve while maximizing your potential to move fast through the straights.

Life throws you curves as well. Too little caution and it can ruin you. Too little efficiency, and you'll come out on the other end very slowly, missing the opportunity to make huge gains in the next economic straightaway. Anyone can make money during economic times like 2005–06, but it was in the curves of 2008–12 that princes were made. Those who saw the curve coming and entered it efficiently—shoring up their spending and divesting themselves of excess financial baggage— were able to open up the throttle when the economy started to boom again in 2013. As Warren Buffett once advised, "Be greedy when people are fearful and fearful when people are greedy." When everyone is careening along at breakneck speed into the inevitable curve, that's the time to be wary of crashes; when everyone is coming out of the curve overly cautious, that's when you pour on the speed and improve your position in the rankings.

One final point about my racing experience. I could have done extensive research to determine the best equipment for myself. I could have taken classes in motorcycle mechanics, taking apart and reassembling motorcycles over and over until I could do it quickly and efficiently. I could have spent many hours studying track records and watching videos for each facility to determine the best lines, breaking points, markers, etc. I could have done research on nutrition and hydration to come up with the optimal dietary supplements. Maybe in five or more years, after all of this research, I would actually get on a motorcycle. Even then, I would only have the benefit of book knowledge rather than experience, so I'd still have a learning curve to navigate on the actual track.

There is one rule that princes know instinctively, and it makes them very different from most other people: *Successful people only do things they are good at or get special joy from.* They focus their time and energy on those things from which they can get excellent return on their investment of time and effort, whether that is a return in dollars or happiness. They hire someone who is exceptionally skilled at the things they don't enjoy or cannot do efficiently. Following this principle requires humility, honesty, and a willingness to admit your weaknesses. The vast majority of people in our country cannot do that. Most people have egos that prevent them from being humble, or greed that stops them from paying someone else to do something that they might be able to muddle through. Big mistake.

I have no interest in becoming a great motorcycle mechanic, a nutritionist, or track statistician. I would not be any good at any of those things. I am, however, good at riding a motorcycle and very good at managing my fears. I hired other people to do the things that I was not good at, and spent my time riding in races. It did not hurt my ego to ask others for help in those areas, because my goal was to be a winner. People with huge egos have a large hurdle to overcome before they can be winners. Sure, they may drive flashy cars and wear expensive clothing, but many of those people have little or no money in the bank. They spend it all every month to assuage their egos, and sacrifice their future for the sake of their present.

A mentor, who is also one of my five closest associates, has said to me on several occasions, "Never try to hide your weaknesses. The people you are trying to hide them from will find out anyway. Instead, be open about your weaknesses and ask for help in areas you need help." Note that he was not talking about personality flaws; he was referring to areas of business where your operation, product, or service is not at its best. He told me this right after he had been to a business meeting with one of the wealthiest men in the country, asking for money to launch a business. That man already had done his research and knew about the weak points in the business plan. He tested my friend by asking leading questions to see if there would be an attempt to hide the truth. It was precisely my friend's openness about those weaknesses that won the support of this investor. The result? He launched a business that is now clicking along at almost $100 million a year in revenue.

LESSON 5:

Look through the curve. Visualize yourself with your goal in hand and go out and get it. Races are won in the curves, where crisis and challenge also represent opportunity. So don't fixate on the inevitable obstacles; set yourself up to exit the curve at the greatest possible speed. Surround yourself with winners whose strengths complement your weaknesses. Successful people only spend their time on things they are good at or get special joy from.

And while you're pursuing your goals, whatever they may be, don't ever forget: The whole point of being on the racetrack, or in the race of life, is to have fun.

CHAPTER 8

Assets and Liabilities

Fully understanding assets and liabilities includes the need to measure the actual impact that your decisions have. It is appropriate to have this discussion after talking about the importance of identifying your one thing, because your one thing should not be simply money or material goods. Why do I say that? Many people might argue that the accumulation of money is precisely what your goal should be, if you want to achieve a secure future. Well, recent stock market history shows that the pursuit of money for money's sake can and does leave people destitute; even if they believed their future was 100% secure. Add to that the staggering roster of people who are fabulously wealthy, but who are miserable, divorced, depressed, addicted to drugs and alcohol, or even suicidal.

The accumulation of money does not equal happiness or success if, in the process, we have alienated our friends and family and become untrue to ourselves and our values.

When Donald Trump measures potential investment opportunities based on a higher purpose, he is really asking, "What is this person's one thing?" What is it that will drive their decisions, keep them at the office late at night, and get them out of bed early in the morning, ready to conquer the world? What do they value?

Put simply, an asset is something that gives, whereas a liability is something that takes. Our one thing is an asset, because that is what gives us the drive, ambition, passion, persistence, and perseverance to accomplish our goals. So, to start with, you could say that the first and most important asset that we acquire is our one thing. It is also very likely that this one thing will be a lifelong pursuit. We need to set, pursue, and achieve a variety of smaller goals—and accumulate smaller assets—along the way. When added up together, they satisfy and enable our one thing.

Here is where many, even most, people run into problems. Our education and culture tell us to pursue things that end up being liabilities, pushing our one thing even further out of reach rather than bringing it closer to us. The miseducation is intentional and malevolent. Period.

What I want you to understand, however, is not just the philosophical position; I also want you to see the purely financial component. Then, I want you to take this basic concept and start applying it to larger and more important financial decisions in your life. So let's look at the facts.

There is a very real practice in American business called *planned obsolescence*. A manufacturer intentionally designs and sells a product at a lesser quality than they are capable of producing. The first way we generally see this is in a technology or electronics product. The seller may not place all of the available upgrades or features in the most current model, because if they did that, then you would not need to buy a replacement soon enough. They intentionally hold back so that they can introduce a new and improved version next year—even though your current version does the job that you bought it for just fine. You must have the newest gadgets (remember, innovation drives need).

The second way that a manufacturer uses planned obsolescence is in making a product that is designed to break down or cease operating properly in a certain period of time to force you to buy a replacement. Yes, it sounds evil, but it is true. Many of the products we buy could be built to have a longer life span, but that would hurt the company's cash flow.

A quick example from my own experience: I purchased a high-end refrigerator for about $2,500 at a time when a mainstream brand could be purchased for around half that. The promise was that this refrigerator was more efficient and would last two or three times as long as the common manufacturer brands, not to mention offering several bells and whistles and a chic design. However, only five or six years into ownership, a plastic piece within the ice maker broke, rendering some of the functions useless. Well, I am a pretty handy guy, so I disassembled the ice maker and took the broken part to the dealer to buy a replacement. Mind you, I also have an engineering background and I know full well that the manufacturing cost of this plastic part could not be more than $25 or $30. Imagine my surprise when the clerk told me that the replacement part would cost almost $600! Naturally, I protested the price, reminding the clerk that an entirely new appliance would only cost three times that amount. The clerk responded by saying, "Sounds like it's time to buy a new refrigerator."

Clearly, the company was not interested in providing service or keeping its models operating. The company had structured its entire business model so that units would break down sooner than the purchase price justified and the cost of repair would force customers to buy more new appliances. First, I did not buy a new model. I went home and fabricated the part myself from sheet metal, extending the life of my refrigerator another six years. Second, that company lost my business forever.

Planned obsolescence is a real and insidious practice that has the potential to trap consumers into a lifetime of servitude. Let's get back to the new car, as an example. We have all heard the advice that you should not let the salesperson talk to you in terms of "what you want your payment to be"—but few people understand why and how falling into this trap has long-lasting repercussions.

The fact is that auto manufacturers and dealers who have their own finance companies can make almost any car affordable to almost any buyer. According to *USA Today* on September 7, 2014, "Experian Automotive says that in the first quarter of 2014, 24.9% of all new-car loans were 73 to 84 months long." Seven years to pay off a car loan? For that matter, how many of us would hold on to a car for seven years before wanting or needing to trade it in? According to the U.S. Department of Transportation's Federal Highway Administration, the average American between the ages of 20 and 54 years old puts more than 15,000 miles per year on a vehicle.

That means that over the course of a seven-year auto loan, the average American will put more than 105,000 miles on a car. (In my case, that expectation is quite low, as I put well over 25,000 miles per year on a vehicle due to the nature of my consulting work.) Worse still, the vast majority of your loan payment in the early years is interest and not principal. After a cycle of buying several cars, the debt carry-forward becomes an oppressive load that can cripple you for your entire life.

Therefore, clearly there are only three ways to win at buying a new car: 1) Make the loan term as short as possible (painfully short, in terms of the payment size) so that the value of the vehicle when it is paid off is high enough to actually subsidize your next purchase; 2) keep the vehicle longer than the term of the loan, and put aside the cash that would have been used for the payment in a savings account toward your next vehicle; or 3) only pay cash for your vehicles, so that you are never hamstrung in the future by the financing snowball.

While that may sound simple, the fact is that new car buying has slowed dramatically in recent years due to low median household incomes. Prior to the Great Recession, the average American purchased a new car every four years. Today, that has slowed to almost a six- or seven-year cycle. Auto manufacturers, who have sharply increased auto prices, are aware of the trend and are responding with ridiculously long finance terms and marketing ploys. In other words, the commercial feudal lords are working to control your aspirations, ideals, and vision of success. A significant part of that strategy is advertising that depicts new car ownership as a symbol of success and intelligence, making a new car look like an asset.

Is a new car, purchased with a seven-year loan, an asset or a liability? Would a properly educated prince make the decision to do that?

Here's another story that may help you cement the answer in your mind.

There is a beautiful hotel in Phoenix, Arizona called the Royal Palms. The hotel has been a favorite destination of celebrities, dignitaries, and presidents since 1948. However, the Royal Palms started its life in the early 1920s as a winter home for New York financier Delos Cooke. What is noteworthy is that, unlike the mansions built during the Gilded Age by the wealthy elite—retreat homes that bled money for the sake of presenting a regal appearance, which are almost all now museums (e.g., Hearst Castle, Biltmore Estate, and Newport (RI) Mansions)—Cooke decided that his new estate needed to be completely self-sustaining. In addition to constructing the home and grounds, he also commissioned a large citrus orchard, which would operate as a commercial business, employing and occupying the staff on a year-round basis. That way, the cost of keeping up the property during the two-thirds of the year when Cooke and his family were not present would not become a cash drain on his other enterprises.

What do we learn from this? Wealthy people—princes—do not buy things that cost them money. They buy things that make them money or they do not buy them at all.

So how do we apply this lesson to the subject of buying a car, an appliance, a vacation home, or a new computer? As to the car: Unless you live in one of the few major cities in the U.S. that has truly adequate public transportation, you need your own transportation to get to work and to be able to take advantage of opportunities. So, if you must buy a car, choose one you can pay off within two or three years and which, at that time, will have enough life left in it to enable you to put away money toward your next car. If you live by this rule, then in a short period of time, you will be able to buy a car for cash—saving yourself all of the interest associated with auto financing and enabling you to put aside more money for the next car and to invest for growth. At some point, and much sooner than you would expect, you will be able to buy that dream car for cash, and then you can have it all! If possible, find a way to start a home business and use your car for that purpose so that you can write the mileage off on your tax return, further reducing the negative cash flow. A car that is purchased based on the long-term finance programs—getting you into a vehicle that you really cannot really afford—is nothing but a liability and a drug. Long-term financing and planned obsolescence are quite literally designed to keep you playing catch-up for the rest of your life.

The principle is no different when it comes to housing. How many people do you know who, during the 2004 through 2007 economic boom—when mortgages were being given to anyone with a pulse—went out and bought a house, or perhaps multiple houses, that they simply could not afford? Were banks and the government encouraging responsible borrowing and purchasing? No. In fact, the very entities that are entrusted to protect our interests were blatantly and decisively positioning the average American to overborrow. These consumers were in a position of almost-certain default, resulting in a decimated credit score followed by years or even decades where that consumer would be forced to borrow at higher interest rates than normal. Call me a conspiracy theorist, but I sincerely believe that the age of NINJA loans (no income, no job, no assets verification) was deliberately designed to destroy the credit scores of middle America so that banks could make more money in the future on high-interest-rate loans.

Don't believe me? Just Google search: "Fannie Mae Debt to Income Ratio." The first link that pops up directs you to a web page of Fannie Mae (the Federal National Mortgage Association). There, you'll see that the acceptable debt-to-income ratio (known as the DTI, i.e., the percentage of your gross annual income which can be used to pay for housing expense) allowed by this federal program is up to a whopping 45%—or even 50% under certain conditions!

Compare that to the Department of Housing and Urban Development Federal Housing Authority (FHA) loan requirements, which specify that the maximum DTI ratio for a qualifying loan is 31%, which must include not only the mortgage payment but also account for property taxes, home insurance costs, homeowner's association dues and, if needed, private mortgage insurance. When I purchased my first home in 1988 with an FHA loan, the maximum allowable DTI was 28% of my gross annual income. How, in less than 20 years, could our government and the banks decide that an acceptable DTI should rise from 28% to 50%? Clearly, the goal of getting people into homeownership was just a shrouded effort to destroy the creditworthiness of middle America, giving banks the ability to charge much higher interest rates for the rest of your lives.

LESSON 6:

The items most people consider assets—such as large homes or expensive cars—are almost always liabilities. The system that sells you on this vision, and gladly finances your purchase, is explicitly designed to get you to overspend, making it very difficult for you to have extra cash to invest. It is also designed to put you at risk of eventually damaging your credit, which enables the banking industry to charge you higher interest rates in the future. Finally, by getting you to engage in a lifestyle in which your self-image and self-worth become measured by excessive and expensive material things, you are being addicted to a drug. You constantly need your next fix and you can begin to make bad decisions in the pursuit of your next fix.

Now, am I saying that you should live like a monk? Of course not. If you have the money, you should enjoy it. What I am saying, however, is that if you really do not have the money and you pursue these things, then you will probably never have any money (i.e., you will remain a pauper). Exercise the self-discipline to buy at your appropriate level at each point in your life.

CHAPTER 9

The Most Important Word

Let's give you some information to loosen things up a bit, so that you can decide what your one thing is with an unfettered mind.

As mentioned previously, I believe math is the most important word in the English language moving forward in American society for the next 30 years or so. Rest assured, you don't need to be a calculus whiz to understand the problems with the numbers.

The baby boomer definition of success is still an enormous part of American social and political dogma, often under the guise of "the American dream." It is so important to our government to keep the hope of this dream alive that Congress passed the Home Affordable Refinance Program (HARP) to assist people in modifying mortgages on homes that they purchased at the wrong time and for probably much more than they could realistically afford. In other words, HARP serves to keep people chained to their mistakes. This program continues to bail out banks long after President Bush gave them $800 billion in 2007, and since President Obama initiated the 2012 Quantitative Easing III policy, which effectively uses federal money to back subprime mortgage loans that Fannie Mae acquired from banks run amok. The point is, the government really wants to keep people in their homes. But don't be duped into thinking this is a purely benevolent act of government to help poor defenseless John Q. Public. This is all a part of a larger policy to keep Americans obsessed with the dream of owning a home, whether it is good for them or not. The baby boomers' desire for a panacea is still at the core of government efforts to control our thinking.

Another important linchpin of federal policy is the entitlement programs that have largely driven the planning of most Americans since the 1930s. Let's look at just one piece of the federal entitlement policy puzzle: Medicare. The baby boomer generation is the largest generational demographic in American history, at a population of about 78 million (more or less, depending on your source). The total population of the United States at the time of this writing is about 320 million. All you need is simple division to see that almost one out of every four people in the country is a baby boomer. So then, how many of those baby boomers are currently enrolled in the Medicare system, which is already struggling to pay its bills? 40%? 50%? 60%?

You may want to sit down for this.

How old do you have to be to draw on Medicare? Age 65. The youngest baby boomer, born on January 1, 1946, turned 65 years old on January 1, 2011—only three years ago. At the time of this writing, only about 26% have attained that age. On average, baby boomers are turning 65 years old at the alarming rate of 11,000 per day for the next 15 years!

What does that mean for the viability of the Medicare system? What about the continued viability of the Social Security system? How long will those government entitlement programs continue to be a helpful and reliable piece of the retirement puzzle? Where is the money going to come from to continue paying these public debts? Well, the answer to that is very simple: The U.S. government keeps printing it. What does that mean? How can we just print money?

During the Nixon administration in the early 1970s, our money was taken off of the gold standard and converted to currency. Prior to that, the law only allowed the government to print legal tender in direct proportion to the amount of gold being held at Fort Knox. Our money had intrinsic, measurable, and redeemable value. After that, our money became currency, meaning that it is backed by promissory notes guaranteed by the federal government. There are checks and balances in the system, yes, which are intended to provide international assurances that the value of our currency is solid—but the strength of these assurances is eroded each and every day, because the government keeps printing more money.

What do you think happens to the value of the dollar in your pocket every time a new dollar is printed? That's right: It goes down! The dollar is worth less today than it was yesterday, and will be worth less tomorrow than it is today—which we call *inflation*. If you listen to policy makers, you may wonder, "Isn't inflation a good thing?" Well, yes and no. The current federal fiscal policy based on an inflation-hungry economy is a result of *Keynesian economics*. Keynesian economics refers to a philosophy developed by British economist John Maynard Keynes in the 1930s. In attempting to understand the Great Depression, Keynes theorized that the failure of continued economic growth, due to the limited marketplace of people with disposable income to purchase consumer goods, represented a fatal flaw in the ability of America to remain in the place of world economic superpower. The solution was to put more money into the hands of more people. In other words, create a middle class. How to do this? This new middle class needed income that would increase with time rather than be stagnant—their jobs needed to pay them more and more as the years went by. In order for employee payrolls to increase, the employers would need to make more money. To make more money, companies would have to be able to charge ever increasing amounts for their goods and services. Prices would always need to climb higher and higher. Increasing prices meant more revenue for companies, which meant higher pay for employees, which meant more disposable household income, which meant that the consumers could afford to buy more and pay more for the goods and services of increasing cost, which meant more revenue for companies, which meant higher pay for employees, which meant more disposable income, and on and on and on. Whew! Thus our country adopted an official policy of supporting and even fostering inflation.

However, the evidence clearly shows that this policy has not played out as intended. Information released by the U.S. Census Bureau in 2013 shows that inflation-adjusted wages in the United States for the lower 95% of our population have not increased since about 1973—and has actually significantly decreased for the bottom 80% of American earners. That means that the middle class has neither experienced an ever-increasing disposable income bucket nor better quality of life. Those of you with a few years under your belt can look back and admit that, for the most part, bigger homes, better cars, and more conveniences are paid for by longer working hours and multiple income households, not pay increases that outpace inflation.

To make the situation worse, the statistics above regarding the number of baby boomers mean that by the end of the next decade, almost one-quarter of our population will be on a fixed income. Note: This assumes that the top 5% of wage earners are not statistically relevant in the context of this discussion, as this group is not large enough to overcome the economic failure of the other 95%. (Does this remind you of the time that preceded the Great Depression?) So, in gross terms, 25% of the people in the U.S. will not be able to participate in the Keynesian model. Add to that the percentage of the population under the age of 18 (23.3%, according to the U.S. Census Bureau) who will not be earning an appreciable income. That means that within the next decade, the growth and strength of the American economy based on current economic policy will be entirely borne by only half of our population. Consider, too, that approximately 45% of that half receive their income directly or indirectly from government—as members of the military, government employees, and disability recipients—and will receive their retirement income from Uncle Sam.

Add it all up. Under a Keynesian economic system, likely at some point within your lifetime, our entire economy will be completely reliant on the disposable income of only one out of four citizens of this country! How will inflation-based growth work then? Will the retirement dreams of our society survive under such circumstances?

Clearly, the answer is no. Your only defense is to extract yourself from the constraints of societal thinking (the retirement propaganda) and forge your own path. That is why—despite all of its issues, failings, and partisanship—America is still the best country in the world to be in at this point in history. Because here, more so than anywhere else in the world, virtually any person with the drive, ambition, and a good idea can start their own business and take their future into their own hands. It does not have to be a large or complicated business, but the tax incentives alone for being an entrepreneur will make a huge difference in your net income—not to mention the opportunity to spend some time and resources doing something that you love or that makes a difference in the world.

LESSON 7:

Seize the day! Everyone (and I mean virtually everyone) should have some sort of business for the tax and enjoyment benefits, whether it is large enough to be your primary source of income or a side operation beyond your normal work schedule or job. Because the government cannot be responsible for your future, you must seize control and pilot your own ship.

CHAPTER 10

Do Your Homework

I am an ardent fan of Robert Kiyosaki and his writing partner, Sharon Lechter, who together wrote the *Rich Dad, Poor Dad* series of books. One of the points they emphasize is that we all have to do our homework. In the context of this book, however, I want to offer a variation on the meaning of that word.

Maybe you have a job that keeps you busy 32 to 40 hours per week—but did you realize that there are 112 waking hours in a week? (Assuming you sleep eight hours per night.) Almost two-thirds of your waking hours are not spent at your regular job. Ask yourself honestly: What do you do with that time? Obviously, we all need to spend time with family, enjoy recreation, and maintain our homes, but when you look at the numbers, does it really make sense that we only spend a third of our waking time on our family's economic maintenance?

In some cases, like my own, the potential disproportion is even greater. I only sleep about five hours a night, sometimes less. Most days, I just can't wait to get out of bed and seize the day's opportunities. In my case, there are about 133 waking hours per week, meaning that a 40-hour-per-week job commands less than a quarter of my conscious time. Every day, it's up to me. Do I use my available time to its maximum potential? Or do I squander it?

As you can see from the above breakdown, most of us have lots of time at our command, to do with what we want. Now we need to be absolutely clear about something. Please note that I did not refer to this as spare time. There is no such thing as spare time. Why? In Chapter 1, I pointed out that we are all faced with a problem, which is that we all have a finite amount of time left on the planet. We also all have the same amount in each day, week, month, or year. Therefore, time is precious, should be guarded jealously, and used wisely. It should not be squandered. To refer to time as spare, by definition, diminishes its value. The law of supply and demand says that anything that is in abundance has less value than anything that is rare. Time—particularly waking hours not earmarked for your job—should be seen as rare and precious. For instance, I had planned to write this book for years, but could never seem to find the time. Recently, my consulting business had me flying across the country several times per month. For the first couple of months, I spent that time napping, watching the in-flight movie, and playing solitaire on my tablet. I began to develop a feeling of dissatisfaction that grew with each flight—and finally realized that it was because I was allowing this time to be squandered. I could not live with that and suddenly realized that this time could be my book writing time. It became so valuable to me that I began to look forward to sitting in a cramped metal tube hurtling through the sky with 250 other surly travelers. Just by changing my thinking and attitude about the potential for this time, my travel went from being wasted time to precious time. This was now time that I was investing: time which I could use to change the lives of countless other people by formulating a message that our country sorely needs to hear.

When I was in my late twenties, I knew a man named Neil L., then in his mid-eighties. I was lucky as a young man to call him a friend. Neil was the man who invented the process of galvanizing steel, which made him very comfortable financially. He had money to spare. What he did not have to spare was time. He understood the extreme value of time and once told me a story about taking his Cadillac into the dealer for service—there was a recall on the vehicle, and he took it in and waited several hours for it to be repaired. Unfortunately, the repair was not done properly and he needed to take the car back in a second time, and then a third time, to get the work done right. The dealership, of course, did not charge him for the work, because it was a recall issue, but on his third visit to the dealer, Neil sat down with the service manager and had a very frank conversation. He told the service manager in no uncertain terms that he expected the car to be serviced correctly and that he did not like being stolen from. The service manager said, "What do you mean? We are performing the work at no cost. We are not stealing from you." Neil responded: "I am 85 years old! I do not have much time left, and you are stealing it from me!"

I will never forget how Neil viewed his time. He hated to spend it nonproductively. Time has value, and we can spend it, save it, invest it, or squander it; and the time we spend not at our job has the highest potential value. Typically, you and your employer have agreed on a fixed value for your time, and you exchange your time for money at that fixed rate. That epiphany, by the way, goes right to the point I have made about our entire economic system being designed to create worker bees, or paupers.

How do you view and use your time? Perhaps you have a second job or run a business on the side. Maybe you are pursuing continuing education in your field, or otherwise improving yourself physically, emotionally, and mentally. These are all good uses of that time, as is reading this book and coming to a deeper understanding of the way the system works against you—if you let it.

We need to make every second count. So think about this: If there is no spare time when you are 30 or 40 years old and have a job but many years ahead of you, why should there be spare time when you are 65 and retired but with far fewer years ahead of you? If time becomes even more precious as we have less of it to spend, I believe we should never reach a point in life where we feel that we do not need to be productive with it. In other words, how do we define—or redefine—retirement? I want you to think about this question, as it goes to the heart of your one thing.

I once complained to a business associate that I really hated going out for lunch during the day, because of time lost waiting in line, waiting for a table, or waiting to be served. I can prepare lunch for myself in a matter of minutes rather than killing an hour while someone else does it for me. My friend became slightly offended, thinking I was voicing a criticism about his values. "But that is just the way things are," he said. "Everyone has to deal with it, why do you think your time is more important than other people's?"

"I don't think my time is more important than anyone else's," I responded. "I just have different priorities than most people. I don't need to have my ego stroked by being served. My priority is to use my time to its highest and best value because, of all the things in life on this earth, time is the one and only thing that I cannot manufacture more of, and that makes it priceless. So, if you do not think your time is as valuable as I think mine is, then that is your problem, not mine."

LESSON 8:

Change your thinking. Choose to be industrious with your available time—because there is no such thing as spare time.

CHAPTER 11

The Rule of 72

The purpose of homework (defined here as work that you make income from that is not from your main job) is to open the door to opportunity. Taking advantage of such an opportunity may require using some of your disposable income to invest and have it grow. That's not an option if you spend every cent of your paycheck. This is a long-term process, not an overnight fix.

A client of mine asked me to sit down with her 20-year-old grandson (named Tyler) and educate him about money and how it works, helping him to create a foundation for good decision making. I asked him, "Do you spend everything you make?" The answer was yes, so we sat down and I helped him create a household budget—his first ever. That's not unusual, however. In my financial-advisory practice, in fact, I have discovered that a large majority of people have never written out their household budgets. In many cases, it is because it makes them accountable to themselves. Most people are afraid of the answer to the question, "What can I truly afford?" Fearing accountability is a quick route to slavery to the commercial system. They choose to be poor. They have the wrong mental attitude, and attitude is everything. As Kiyosaki says, "Broke is temporary…Poor is permanent." There's a big difference between having no money and lacking the self-control to improve your financial situation.

Once Tyler and I prepared his household budget, we were able to identify several regular expenses that were frivolous. We earmarked this money for saving and investing. Then we discussed whether or not he would do his homework. He was more interested in passive investing, not actively managing the monetary growth. Under those circumstances, we decided that a reasonable goal for annual rate of return for him without too much risk would be no more than 6%. Then I walked him through the math. I taught him about the *Rule of 72*, which helps calculate the effect of compounding interest. Albert Einstein, when once asked what he thought was the most powerful force on earth, did not mention the atom or any of the laws of physics. He said, "Compound interest is the eighth wonder of the world. He who understands it, earns it—he who doesn't, pays it."

Here is how the Rule of 72 works: Take the interest rate that you are making on your money and divide that into the number 72. The resulting number is how many years of compounding that it will take for your money to double in value.

Let's say you had $100,000 and were earning an interest rate of 2%. Seventy-two divided by 2% equals 36 years. That means that at an interest rate of 2%, which is more than you can get in a bank CD today, it will take 36 years for your $100,000 to become $200,000. Thirty-six years! What does this tell us? That we have to make a better rate of return. So, I talked Tyler through a scenario where he made an interest rate of 6%.

"OK, if you cut the corners we discussed, then you can save $150 per month or $1,800 per year," I said. "According to the Rule of 72, your money will double in value every 12 years (72/6=12). Every 12 years, your first $1,800 of principal will double in value and become worth $18,510 when you reach age 60. The same thing happens with each successive year's principal, only it has one less year to mature, so your second year's $1,800 principal will be worth $17,466 when you reach age 60. Each year, your additional principal grows and is added to the pot. At the end of the day, when you reach age 60, you will have saved and invested a total of $73,800…but the compounded value of that investment, at 6% interest, will be a whopping $297,086…four times the principal investment!" What a great start to a retirement plan that even a 20-year-old could afford to implement! Both Tyler's grandmother and I were pleased and proud that he started his retirement plan immediately—that very same day!

Now, I realize that waiting 40 years seems a ridiculously long time—but, once again, it's math. The Rule of 72 is an important lesson that may very well determine whether you are a prince or a pauper.

If you are a prince with plenty of money, then investments that generate a predictable compounding rate of return—without risk to principal—should be in your financial plan. Let's say your investments are allocated 50% into fixed instruments with low or no risk and 50% into variable products with greater risk. If you were to suddenly lose all of your risky money due to a worldwide economic meltdown, then half of your money would be protected. After compounding, you would be whole again in seven to 10 years. In the financial industry, we call it *sleep insurance*, because you won't ever lose sleep over the prospect of being financially ruined.

If you are not a prince, and have very limited resources, then you obviously cannot afford to lose what you have—and understanding the Rule of 72 is your first building block. You should utilize fixed and guaranteed financial instruments until you have enough money to reasonably secure your future. Only then you can afford to put some money in higher-risk investments—with the possibility of doubling to tripling your money in relatively shorter periods of time, but only risking the money that you can afford to lose.

By the way, even in today's environment, there are investments that make up to, and even in excess of, 6% interest without incurring risk. Your broker may say that is not possible, but it is, and I help many of my clients do just that.

LESSON 9:

Prepare a budget for yourself, and be fearless and thorough in its preparation. No matter how much money you make, be determined to not spend it all. Diligently set aside money that you can nurture and grow, using the power of compounding to secure your future. Start as early as you can—because time is your friend when relying on compounding. If you do not have a lot of time in front of you, use the Rule of 72 to hedge yourself against financial ruin and only use the money you can afford to lose to try to make dramatic improvements to your situation.

CHAPTER 12

Risk vs. Reward

Because everyone's situation, risk tolerance, long-term needs, legacy planning, and other factors are vastly different, this book is not the place to offer recommendations on specific financial products. I can, however, offer you this additional piece of education: There are only two kinds of investments. I am discussing this now, because it has a direct relationship to your success in using the Rule of 72. Before you start thinking that you're diversified into far more than two different kinds of investments, let me explain.

The two kinds of investments are: *fixed* and *variable.* There are hundreds of different investment vehicles and thousands of different products that may seem to represent numerous kinds of investments. With only a few exceptions, however, they all fall into these two categories.

Well, the definition of the word variable is that the risk belongs to the account holder, while the definition of the word fixed is that the risk belongs to the financial institution or company that is the custodian of the account. In other words, if you have money invested in products that can go up or down in value, and the gain or loss is reflected in your account value, then the risk belongs to you as the account holder. In contrast, if you have money invested in products where the value of your account can never go down—regardless of what happens to the specific holding that your money has purchased—then the risk belongs to the financial institution; they are guaranteeing your account value. Notice that I did not say you would make money in your fixed investment, because a guaranteed rate of return may or may not be a part of the specific investment vehicle. What makes it fixed is that your principal is guaranteed to be protected from any losses.

Examples of variable investment products include:
- stocks
- bonds
- mutual funds
- exchange traded funds (ETFs)
- real estate investment trusts (REITs)
- deeded real estate
- stock options
- variable annuities
- variable life insurance policies
- gold and jewelry, collectibles, etc.

Any and all of these products have the potential to go up in value (sometimes quite dramatically), but also have the potential to go down in value (sometimes equally dramatically). Note that if your broker has your savings allocated into stocks, bonds, mutual funds, and REITs, and is telling you that you are diversified, that is simply not true. Recent history tells us that all of these investment vehicles can lose money in a big way, all at the same time, which can wipe you out!

Examples of fixed investment products are:
- U.S. Treasury bills
- bank certificates of deposit (CDs)
- bonds
- fixed annuities
- fixed indexed annuities
- secured debentures

Any and all of these products are guaranteed not to lose principal—provided that you play by the rules. For instance, a CD will not lose principal, provided you deposit your funds with an FDIC-insured bank and your deposit amount is no greater than the FDIC insurance limit (currently $250,000 per deposit account per bank). A fixed or fixed indexed annuity is guaranteed not to lose principal value, provided you do not withdraw more than the surrender-charge-free amount in a calendar year and your deposit does not exceed the State Guarantee Fund account limit. Of course, all of these fixed products that guarantee principal offer those guarantees in the form of your contract with the custodian and whatever underlying insurance is offered, such as Federal Deposit Insurance coverage. The truth is there are no absolute guarantees in life. Global nuclear war might wipe out the government's ability to honor FDIC insurance, so if that happens, you're out of luck. But I would think that in such an event, your CD balance would not be the foremost thing on your mind.

Now, you may notice that I have listed bonds in both the variable and the fixed categories. Why is that? Because bonds are unique in that they are fixed (protected) if held to term, but they can also be bought or sold during their term—and this happens quite often. The strength of their principal guarantee is also derived from the strength of the entity that issues the bond, so the word *guarantee* can have nuances. So let's just take a minute to understand how bonds work.

A bond is a contract under which you loan your money to either a government entity, such as the familiar war bond or a municipal improvement district bond, or a quasi-governmental entity, such as a utility or a college, or to a commercial endeavor, such as a private company. The entity agrees to pay a specified interest rate on your loan called the *coupon rate*. Generally, the contract is illiquid, in the respect that you cannot terminate it early; but the good news is that if you play by the rules, meaning you hold the bond to term, the coupon rate is fixed and guaranteed, in accordance with the strength of the borrowing entity. Under these circumstances, a bond can be considered a fixed investment vehicle. Most bonds are structured to have fairly long terms, however, and many bondholders are not willing or able to hold the bond to maturity. In such a case, the owner of the bond can sell it on the bond market just like a stock holding, but the return, or sale price, is affected by many factors and may pay more or less than the coupon rate.

For example: You hold a 20-year Federal Class EE bond with a coupon rate of 5%, and after 10 years decide you want to convert the contract into cash. You can sell it, with the buyer paying a rate based on the anticipated yield of the remainder of the contract term. But, what happens if you try to sell your bond during a bull market, where the Dow Jones Industrial Average has been making 8% per year for the past few years and still looks strong? There's not going to be much appetite for a 5% annual rate of return when you can make 8% or better. The law of supply and demand says that you will have to discount the bond if you want to sell it. Conversely, let's say you were trying to sell your bond yielding a 5% coupon rate for the next 10 years in 2008, when the Dow had recently lost 65% of its value and the world economy showed no signs of quick recovery? A guaranteed return looked pretty good to an investor by comparison and the higher demand might have enabled you to sell the remaining contract period for a premium. As you can see from these examples, a bond can go up or down in value, making it variable; moreover, if the bond is issued by an entity other than the federal government, the strength of the principal guarantee may not be as solid as some other fixed instruments.

LESSON 10:

No matter what your income is, find a way to start saving money. Don't put it off just because the time horizon for success looks to be long. Fixed investments should be part of everyone's financial plans. Stocks, bonds, and mutual funds are not a diversified portfolio. Once you have a basic budget and are funding your savings account regularly—and that account is structured to offer some degree of protection for your future—then you can start utilizing more risky investments. No matter where you are in life, get started!

CHAPTER 13

The Show Must Go On

Retirement propaganda has left too many people devastated in its wake over the past 50 years. There are two components of the psychology of the American public that each of us, as individuals, must face up to. Indeed, these two psychological factors will almost certainly ensure that the majority of our population will exist as paupers, no matter what their apparent work ethic.

The first has to do with our appetite for learning.

We must have an educational transformation if we truly desire the opportunity to become princes instead of paupers. Earlier, I talked about the life vision that has been foisted upon Americans by the commercial and educational system, which locks people into a buy-and-hold mindset. Generally this phrase has been linked to stock market investment, but this same mental predisposition has also locked people into a lifelong struggle to recoup their investment into their mainstream education.

Let's face it, college and/or technical education is big business, and the cost of higher education has skyrocketed in the past 30 years. To give you some perspective, the National Center for Education Statistics indicates the average cost of a four-year college degree (both private and public institutions) in 1976–1977 was $2,577 per year. In 2014–2015, 38 years later, that same education cost $31,374 per year, according to *USA Today* (including room and board). That equates to a compounded annual average inflation rate of just under 7% per year for higher education. During the same period, the CPI (consumer price index) increase has been only 3.86% per year on average. Moreover, when you consider that the average cost of a three-bedroom home in the U.S. is approximately $175,000, we begin to see this so-called education investment in context. Many Americans are leaving college with a student debt burden nearly equal to the cost of a home mortgage. Think about it: What story could big business and big college be selling that would drive the American public to pay those kinds of disproportionate inflation rates?

It is the same advice that drives many Americans into a life of servitude: the buy-and-hold philosophy. In other words, you might be willing to pay such an exorbitant price for your education if you believed that you would have at least 40 working years to pay it off, and that the return on this investment was an ability to earn a significantly higher annual income than you would otherwise have without it.

The problem is that we live in the most dynamic economy in history. This means that, due to rapidly changing technology, a product or service which is all the rage today can be completely obsolete in just a few short months or years. The skills that were required to produce or service that need become obsolete with that product. Additionally, every day our economy becomes more and more global, which means that there is an ever-increasing workforce capable of filling these rapidly transforming jobs at lower and lower wages.

Why am I bringing all of this up? It may sound like I am attacking the highly advertised need for a college education, but that is not so, at all. In fact, part of the larger economic problem in America is that our population is becoming less and less competitive with other nations' better-educated workforces.

The connection between the high cost of education (and the American belief that such an investment will pay for itself over a lifetime) is misleading to many of our population. Perhaps it would be more accurate to say that this sales pitch has enabled many of us to become mentally lazy and entitled. That sounds pretty harsh, but it is the truth. Statistics published by the U.S. Department of Labor's Bureau of Labor Statistics show that the average American will hold 11.7 different jobs by the age of 50. This means that there is a good chance you will need to significantly change the direction of your career path several times during your life. For many people, the thought of changing jobs even once in a lifetime is daunting or even terrifying, much less the thought of changing your entire career direction. It's about as far as you can get from the American dream of graduating college and working for an employer that provides a pension plan and job security. In fact, pensions are almost nonexistent in American business culture anymore.

So what does this mean for you? It all goes back to education and how we each individually view it. The transient nature of desirable skills may drive the need to learn an entirely new vocation several times during your life. For many people, education represents a relatively short chapter in their life story—they pay dearly for it and are glad to get through so that they can coast on the achievement. They apply whatever skills they have learned to their job over a long period of time and for many, many people, they stop learning. I would go so far as to say that many people that I have met even resent the concept of learning new skills later in their working life—because they feel that their investment is not paying off adequate dividends for a long enough period of time. During the Great Recession of 2008 through 2012, I knew people who lost their jobs and refused to look for work in career paths that were not in the same field. Some said that moving into a different line of work was "not in their comfort zone," which is really just another way of saying that they simply did not want to learn a new set of skills. They preferred to stay on unemployment out of resentment: How dare the worldwide economy change what it needs from me?

If you happen to be one of those people, there's an important lesson here. It may not be comfortable, but you can learn to improve your lot in life and change your future. We must never stop changing and growing. Rather than resenting the need to learn and adapt, we really need to recognize that it is more important than ever to embrace this reality. You will almost certainly need to reinvent yourself many times during your life. With each reinvention, opportunities will present themselves that can be life-altering in a positive way. With each reinvention, you are better positioned to capitalize on such opportunity, because your perspective becomes ever broader and more inclusive.

With each reinvention, you move further back away from the trees, so that the forest becomes clearer.

The anecdotal evidence is everywhere around us, but we have to recognize it as the harbinger of truth that it is. When people tell you of their experience, listen closely and try to see how the complete portrait of your own perspective on life is enhanced by the anecdote. Because I travel a lot, I regularly get a chance to chat with people from all walks of life, all business backgrounds, and all parts of the country. I have spoken with dozens of people in just the past few months who have told me that their industry—whether it is healthcare, or engineering, or construction, or technology—is projecting a huge void in competent, skilled workers in the very near future. In many cases, I have heard people lament that their company has already had a severely depleted pool of talent for many years.

How can it be that, when only three years ago, unemployment in the United States was at a "true" level of around 18%, there are industries crying out for qualified applicants? It is because that huge percentage of our population was either unable or unwilling to reinvent themselves and be positioned for the jobs that were available and in demand.

Further evidence of this can be extrapolated from the recent decrease in median household income in the U.S. According to MarketWatch.com, the U.S. Census Bureau reports that the median U.S. household income fell from $56,436 in 2007 to $51,939 in 2013. Why is there an 8% decrease in the median household income in the U.S., when Drexel University has projected an increase of 28% for certain high-tech jobs' starting salaries in roughly that same period of time? Clearly, workers in their 40s and 50s, who should be in their peak earning years, are not able to be employed at their highest and best use. Changing technology is requiring a near-constant infusion of new and current education and the majority of our population is simply not pursuing it. I personally know a number of people who spent the first 10 or 15 years of their working lives in one field, but have not, either during or after the recession, been able to secure replacement employment in that same field and have now been relegated to a lower level of employment. This is not just a tragedy for those individuals and their families; it is a tragedy for our country that these great minds are not being utilized at their highest capacity. While there have been recent times when almost no amount of effort was enough to secure employment at one's highest level, moving forward, we cannot place the blame on the economy, or the government, or even greedy big business.

At some point, we each must take responsibility for our own futures, and come to grips with the absolute demand and necessity to regularly reinvent ourselves. That means learning new skills, or securing new or enhanced training and education to keep us competitive. We also need to keep an open mind to the notion that such evolution is not only not to be resented, but even embraced and sought out to ensure greater success in our future.

I contend that your success in becoming a prince requires that you become an entrepreneur—though not necessarily by the usual definition. Many people think that an entrepreneur is some wildly creative risk taker whose mind functions differently from the average person's mind. That is only partly true. Yes, the mind of an entrepreneur may work differently than yours does, but mainly in this way: An entrepreneur sees and embraces the need to constantly learn new skills in order to be able to take advantage of new opportunities or ideas. This person is not afraid to make mistakes; as long as you don't make the same mistake again, it will make you more successful. A mistake becomes a lesson learned and is simply a part of your education. This person is not afraid to spend time learning something new, even if that particular venture does not play out as expected, because each and every new thing learned enhances one's ability to capitalize on future opportunities. True, some mistakes come at a price; when you consider that one way or another you are going to pay for your education, then a mistake takes on a completely different emotional context and is no longer to be feared. In other words, an entrepreneur embraces the truth that constant learning and reinvention will ultimately lead to success. We may not quite know where or when, but we have faith.

Think how different this perspective is from what the mainstream educational system teaches. You pay to learn a specific vocation with the express goal of being paid back with interest from that specific vocation. If you need to learn a new vocation, then your investment was a failure. Nothing could be further from the truth. Whatever level of education you have received, it is but one piece of the puzzle that, when completed, can portray a beautiful image of the future—but only if all of the pieces are put in their place. During your life, there will be many pieces to sort and place. Don't be afraid or resentful of the many pieces. Seek them out, for the more receptive you are to putting together the puzzle, the quicker your portrait will come into focus.

The second point goes beyond our appetite for learning.

As a nation, we have been brainwashed to believe that our work and our personal lives must be completely separate: It is the separation of those two things, rather than the integration, that spells happiness and success. This philosophy really took root during and after the Industrial Revolution; in the context of human existence, it is an infant philosophy that has not proven to be sustainable. Prior to that time, if you were, say, a farmer, you were not a farmer just between 8 a.m. and 5 p.m. You were a farmer 24 hours a day. In the spring, your workday may have been 16 hours long for four to six weeks to get the fields planted, and again in the fall harvest season; the crops would not wait for your regular hours before rotting off of the vines. However, during the off seasons, you may have needed to work only four hours a day while nature took its course. Likewise, if you were a fisherman, your workday may have been long when the weather permitted, but short when the weather was foul. If you were a merchant, you were always open to making sales or conducting business. This notion we have in our country that you are only at work eight hours a day and the other 16 hours a day are not to be infringed upon—particularly with the dirty business of earning a living—is counterproductive to your long-term interests.

You may contend that it is better now, with regular working hours, so that your leisure time is uninterrupted. In some respects, it's a pleasant luxury. But, we are here to talk about what it takes to be a prince, not an average American worker. The average 9-5 worker may enjoy that relative freedom in the present, but they will also most likely never enjoy the financial independence that the top 1% or 2% of our population enjoys. If your goal is to become one of these princes, then you must adopt their thinking.

In my profession, and among my close associates, I rub elbows with many people who enjoy the true freedom that financial independence offers. I can tell you without hesitation or reserve that among these millionaires and multimillionaires, not one of these people has regular office hours.

That does not mean that they find themselves chained to a desk 20 hours a day. Quite the opposite. They are free to spend much of their time doing things that they love and enjoy. But they are also "always on." Their minds never really shut off. They are at work mentally, even when they are not so physically. That does not mean that work is an overwhelming preoccupation that robs them of the other joys of life, but it does mean that their conscious and their subconscious are always open to the moments that have the power to change their lives.

I call it them *Archimedes moments*, after the ancient Greek mathematician. The legend goes that the king commissioned a very elaborate gold crown be made for himself and provided the raw gold to the craftsman who was engaged for the task. Upon receipt of the finished crown, the king, while very pleased with the work, wondered if all of the gold he had provided was actually used to make the crown. Could some of it have been skimmed off the top by the craftsman? The king hired Archimedes to determine the answer. Unfortunately, the solution eluded Archimedes because the design of the crown was so intricate that there was virtually no way to measure the volume of the gold precisely. Weighing the crown was not the answer, because the craftsman might have inserted a lead core to make up for the lost weight of any stolen gold. How could Archimedes solve this puzzle? The answer came to him one evening while he was relaxing in a bathtub. He noticed that as he lowered himself into the water, the level of the water in the tub rose. He realized that, while the crown might be too intricate to measure with instruments, the amount of water displaced by the crown could be measured to determine the volume of material in the crown. This principle of displacement became known as the *Archimedes principle* in the scientific community. In the realm of your financial education, however, what I call an Archimedes moment is key to understanding the value of always being on. Archimedes solved his work-related problem while engaging in a relaxing activity—taking a bath. His mind was on his work problem, even though his conscious focus was not.

Have you ever wondered why people in high-level business positions go play golf during the workday? Are they neglecting their responsibilities? Not at all. It is often in times of distraction when problems are solved and opportunities are realized. Personally, I cannot count the number of times when I have resolved serious business issues while sailing, riding my motorcycle, or taking a hike.

One of the most important business deals that I ever put together was done during a day on the ski slopes: I made phone calls while taking the lift up to the peak and thought through the mechanics of the deal on the run down the slope.

A final point to the idea that "the show must go on" is that everything we do, say, and think is an indicator of our overall direction in life. There are no small things.

You've likely known many people over the years who live by the mantra, "I don't sweat the small stuff." They justify wasting time watching television because it is "just an hour or so." They excuse occasional misuse of their precious resources by saying that they deserve to splurge once in a while—even if doing so puts them behind on their bills, drives up their credit card balances, or delays being able to find some disposable cash to invest rather than squander. Whether it is time, money, brainpower, or relationships, everything you do, say, and think adds up to the potential for your future. Small things are an indication of what your heart wishes to do in larger things, and so it truly does pay in the long run to be faithful to your one thing in little decisions as well as big decisions.

LESSON 11:

People who earn at the highest levels never really shut down their work or their growth. They are always learning, applying new skills, and realizing new ways of looking at things. They do not segregate education into just one period of their life or work into just one block of hours in the day. They are always on. Because they are multitaskers and are always working in the background, when opportunity does present itself, they are keen to it. They would never overlook something because of some propagandistic aversion to work and education except within certain confines. They are diligent in all respects to the execution of their life goals. They are like method actors, totally invested in their characters, assuming their identities without reserve. Players on a stage who are always ready for the show to go on—and never allow any excuse for nonperformance.

CHAPTER 14

Tell Me Who Your Friends Are...

...and I will tell you who you are. There is a very real and tangible ring of truth to this observation. We are influenced by our associates. The one aspect that I don't like about this particular saying is that it is reactive instead of proactive. In other words, it assumes that you have already made your choice of associates and that, as a result, your path is set. You are already judged.

I prefer a sentiment that I think is more proactive. It goes like this: "You are the average of your five closest associates."

Do you think for a moment that members of al Qaeda would be able to exercise their own conscience and refrain from terrorist activities while they are in the company of other terrorists? Would you likely be able to talk about world politics, national economic policy, philanthropy, or environmental initiatives in a group of people whose favorite TV show is *Here Comes Honey Boo Boo*? In contrast, think about how your mind would be stimulated if your attention was reserved for entrepreneurs, business owners, public servants, and the like? Make no mistake: Lesson number 11 is key to your success if you want to change your station in life.

Why is this an important concept to grasp? It's similar to that old saying that you should dress for the job you want, not the job you have. There are two active components of this little piece to the puzzle. One is internal while the other is external.

The internal component is in making a commitment to yourself. What we are talking about here is literally sitting down and examining your friendships, associations, business contacts, and how you spend your recreational time, and, where needed, making decisive changes.

Say you grew up in a small town in the Midwest. While in high school, you were more concerned with having a good time than making good grades. You barely finished school and work at the local gas station. You spend your time at work with people whose story is more or less like yours, and on your off hours, you also hang out with people who work in minimum-wage jobs. Sure, you talk about doing something different and improving your lot in life, but your circle of friends cannot offer any meaningful advice; they themselves are trapped in essentially the same spider hole. What are the chances you are going to find yourself in significantly different circumstances 10 years later? Probably not too good. Of course there are examples of people who were propelled into a different life, mostly not due to their own designs. But you are reading this book because you want to maximize your chances, not hope for the one-in-10-million shot.

If you want to move up the economic food chain, one of the first things you will need to do is to examine your associates and, where appropriate, change them to associates who will propel you toward your goal.

To be clear, I am not advocating shifting loyalties, being disingenuous, or being manipulative. I am talking about seeking out and truly investing in relationships with people who will help you become the person that you want to become. This takes time and effort. People of quality seek out people of quality, and generally are sensitive to someone who is being false. It will be difficult for you to break into a new circle of friends unless you are genuinely interested and bring something of value to the relationship yourself. This process takes years and is ever evolving.

Just for your reference, I'll give you a list of my five closest associates, so that you get the sense of what I mean:

1. A Yale Law School graduate who practiced international litigation for 20 years, managed a multibillion-dollar hedge fund for one of the largest custodians in the country, taught constitutional law at Princeton University, and currently owns and presides over a $100-million-dollar-a-year company.

2. A surgeon who owns several private surgical centers. She performs both elective and non-elective surgeries, including providing services to celebrities in Beverly Hills, owns and manages an international health and aging management practice, is the author of a very meaningful and insightful wellness book, and is currently producing a documentary movie on the long-term effect of chemical warfare on residual populations as a philanthropic endeavor.

3. An international intellectual property law attorney who also owns and operates a boutique guest ranch, owns a cattle operation that yields several million dollars a year in naturally raised beef, and wrote a business management book which, several years ago, shaped my own business operations in a very material way, aiding my own success.

4. A real estate developer who has developed hundreds of millions of dollars in real estate assets during his career and has been a founding shareholder in a national bank. He is currently working in a consulting capacity for the Canadian government on a large partially subsidized housing project in Alberta, Canada.

5. A former chief operations officer of a $200-million-a-year resort company. She currently operates her own independent business and personal growth consulting firm, where she engages business leaders in a monthly think-tank-style forum that I'm a member of. It's designed so our shared experiences and backgrounds can help each other to bring both business interests and personal lives to the next level of excellence. Her moderation of our discussions ensures surgical precision of our efforts, so that the maximum benefit is realized for the least amount of time and energy.

I consider each of these people to be close friends, mentors, and colleagues, with whom I am able to share intimate thoughts, personal struggles, exciting ideas and ideals, and whose counsel and encouragement I value in the extreme. They are also people with whom I offer observations and advice that they, in turn, value and benefit from. Our relationship is symbiotic.

How is it that this kid from a New England town, whose father wanted him to ride on the back of a city garbage truck, has surrounded himself with such an outstanding group of people? Let me borrow the words of the late Zig Ziglar, renowned author, motivational speaker, and consummate sales professional. He said, "You can have everything out of life that you want, if you just help enough other people get what they want." How true that is.

The core principle of this lesson is that you must surround yourself with people who will elevate you, not bring you down. If you want to get better at basketball, play with people who are better than you are. If you want to get better at business, associate with people who are more successful than you are. If you want to be smarter about money management, retirement, or personal enrichment, then you must associate with people who are smarter, richer, and more sophisticated than you are.

If you want to cultivate a relationship with a person who operates at a higher level than you, I refer you back to Zig. Find a way to help them get something they want. In other words, bring value to them.

I want to be very clear about what I mean. I am not saying that you should suck up to people, or that you should be disingenuous or deceitful. In fact, I would say that any effort at being untrue about your intentions toward such a relationship will prove counterproductive.

People can sense when a snake-oil salesman is talking to them. Moreover, I am not encouraging you to develop a relationship focused on getting a specific thing from someone, and then discarding them once you have what you want. It's not a quid-pro-quo arrangement, exchange, or business transaction. It's about genuine friendship. Remember, the purpose here is to surround yourself with regular associates whose mere presence will elevate your thinking, activities, and aspirations. This is about a process of absorption and it will take time for you to see results in your own metamorphosis.

Ultimately, it comes down to finding a way to bring value to other people's lives. Seek out opportunities to enhance that person's interests and well-being—without seeking anything in return. In pop vernacular, that is called *paying it forward*—and in scriptural terms, "casting your bread upon the water." Find a way to enhance their lives or their business interests, seeking nothing in return, other than the opportunity to spend some time with them. Absorb their energy, their intellect, and their values. In time, you will begin to see yourself changing to become more like them in your thinking and predispositions. That is the goal: to change your thinking. In doing so, you'll open the door to opportunity.

I should also clarify that these five are not my only associates. The same principle can be applied in numerous aspects of your life. I also have five closest associates whose company I hope helps me elevate my spiritual perspective on life. I have five closest associates within my family, from whom and with whom I share experiences that enrich my home life and the quality of my marriage and relationship with my daughter.

These closest associates in different categories of my life may or may not be the same. That really depends on what my goals and aspirations are spiritually, socially, economically, and in areas of personal growth.

Can you work with more than five? It is possible, but my personal experience is that it's difficult to find as many as five people whose personalities, ambitions, character traits, and values will enhance my own. It is also difficult to offer appropriate attention and value to more than five other people in one aspect of life and still be truly genuine and enhance their lives as much as you hope their association can enhance yours.

LESSON 12:

You are the average of your five closest associates. This is a law of nature that is no more avoidable than the law of gravity. Seek out associates whose presence will help you to change your thinking and predispositions. This is a process of change and personal enrichment that is a goal unto itself. These associates are not doorways to a specific opportunity, but rather are catalysts to help you recognize and respond to what the universe offers to each and every one of us: the chance to improve ourselves and our lots in life.

CHAPTER 15

I'd Rather Be Lucky...

Richard Wiseman, a psychologist at the University of Hertfordshire, England, performed a study several years ago to determine why some people seem to be luckier than others. Perhaps you know someone like this. They seem to fall into situations that offer great opportunity, everything they touch seems to turn to gold, and they always seem to be happy and buoyant about whatever life has to offer. You look at them and the only explanation you can come up with is that they seem to have an abundance of good luck, mojo, and karma. You're not just imagining it: Dr. Wiseman's study found that there is a measurable difference in the luck that some people seem to enjoy as compared to others.

Dr. Wiseman's research revealed that lucky people generate good fortune via four basic principles:

1. They are skilled at creating and noticing chance opportunities.
2. They make lucky decisions by listening to their intuition.
3. They create self-fulfilling prophesies via positive expectations.
4. They adopt a resilient attitude that transforms bad luck into good.

I am not superstitious, nor do I believe in actual luck, but the results of this study are empirical, measurable, and documented. So what is going on here—and is there a way that you, I, or anyone else can alter our experience so that we can participate in such good mojo? The answer is yes!

Again, in his article published in the *UK Telegraph*, Dr. Wiseman notes:

- "Unlucky people often fail to follow their intuition when making a choice, whereas lucky people tend to respect hunches. Lucky people are interested in how they both think and feel about the various options, rather than simply looking at the rational side of the situation. I think this helps them because gut feelings act as an alarm bell—a reason to consider a decision carefully."

- "Unlucky people tend to be creatures of routine. They tend to take the same route to and from work and talk to the same types of people at parties. In contrast, many lucky people try to introduce variety into their lives. For example, one person described how he thought of a color before arriving at a party and then introduced himself to people wearing that color. This kind of behavior boosts the likelihood of chance opportunities by introducing variety."

- "Lucky people tend to see the positive side of their ill fortune. They imagine how things could have been worse."

By those measures, I have to say that I experience great luck all the time. Fantastic opportunities open up to me on an almost daily basis. In fact, it is sometimes difficult to choose which opportunity I want to put my time and resources into, because there are so many great options on the table. Let me give you just a couple of examples of how applying the principles of attracting luck have touched me.

As discussed above, one of my five closest associates facilitates a group of local business leaders and entrepreneurs in the metro Phoenix area. She invited me to attend her group meetings, which last for a three-hour period once per month. My initial reaction was that blocking out three hours for a non-revenue-producing meeting was just not a good idea. I believed that I probably did not bring enough to the table in terms of my own personal experience and credentials, and that I would feel embarrassed to participate. I found it hard to comprehend how sitting in on such a group—with wildly diverse business backgrounds—could offer specific benefits to my own business interests in a direct and tangible way. In other words, my initial reaction was a list of reasons why I could not or should not participate.

It was strange, really. I have spent my entire life trying to be open to opportunity, and yet my initial reaction was driven by fear, doubt, and anxiety—a reluctance to open myself up to luck or good fortune. Sadly, the vast majority of people operate in an atmosphere of doubt and fear; an atmosphere of bad karma, if you will. This affects our thinking and our actions. It places a wall between us and opportunity. It also becomes a self-fulfilling prophecy, because, if you operate under the assumption that doing something out of the norm will likely result in a bad outcome, it does. (Not because the actual outcome is truly bad, but because your perception of it is tainted.) You could have the most wonderful experience of your life, but you can only see the bad in it—because that is what you have trained your mind to look for.

So here I was, faced with the invitation to engage with a group of strangers and openly discuss my personal and professional hopes, aspirations, challenges, successes, and failures. My initial reaction was to recoil and protect myself. I have trained myself, however, to recognize the predisposition to bad karma and act contrary to it. So, instead of saying no, I said yes.

The good luck was practically instant. At one of the meetings, the guest speaker was an individual who had a dramatic impact on my life before I even met him. Mike Lechter was the author of a fabulous book called *Other People's Money*, which details a business philosophy of capitalizing on resources that are owned and paid for by other people to enable growth and prosperity in your own business ventures. (By the way, I highly recommend that you buy this book, and read it as a companion to this one.)

During the meeting, Lechter didn't discuss his legal practice or his writing, but rather his hobby business—a guest ranch—and its challenges and obstacles to success. After the forum meeting, I approached him and, following the rule of Lesson 11, introduced myself. I told him how much I admired him and how his book had changed my life. I also told him that I am on the board of directors of a resort hotel in Sedona, Arizona, and that I would be pleased to spend some time with him letting him pick my brain for anything he might find useful to help his business grow. We set up a lunch meeting and I have had the tremendous good luck of developing a meaningful friendship with him. (He subsequently became associate number three.) What have I gotten out of the deal? The opportunity to spend some time with a man who is more educated, more entrepreneurial, a higher thinker in many ways, and better traveled than I am. I have the opportunity to potentially absorb something from the relationship that may help me at some point in the future. What exactly, I can't say, but I say this with absolute assurance: My life, my luck, and my ability to capitalize on future opportunity will be better for having reached out to this man.

LESSON 13:

Be open to the universe and the universe will respond generously. Work diligently to train yourself to act out of hope and joy rather than fear and pain. Robert Kiyosaki says that most people do not take advantage of opportunity because they are afraid of making a mistake—but the truth is that mistakes are a good thing! If you make a mistake, especially a costly one, it becomes very unlikely that you will ever make that same mistake again, increasing the probability that your next venture will be successful. What we are after here is the end result: setting up ourselves, our children, and grandchildren to be princes instead of paupers. There's no need to dwell too much on the bumps in the road.

CHAPTER 16

The Tide Brought Me a Sail

Turn on the television on any given day, and you'll surely see an infomercial in which some real estate guru or investor advertises their sure-fire method for getting rich quick. You'll be promised visions of transforming your life, retiring to a tropical island, or a grand and lavish lifestyle—with little or no effort or investment on your part.

We live in a society where hard work is disdained and people feel entitled to an easy life. This vision has been fostered and cultivated by the princes of society, whether commercial leaders or politicians. The pursuit of wealth and luxury is a powerful motivator that coerces good, honest-hearted people into taking risks that can have ruinous effects.

Ask yourself: If there is so much easy money to be made by flipping houses or investing, why isn't this person doing that, instead of trying to sell the method to me? The truth is, the only person getting rich quick is the person selling the method—not the hapless sheep buying into a business model they know little or nothing about.

Why am I starting this closing chapter with such a scalding message? Because it's possible you still believe that there is a formula, system, or book out there—even this one—that could teach you how to get rich quick! But, what we have discussed so far in this book is more valuable and more important than a system. My expectation is more humble than telling you how to get rich quick; I can help you change your perspective, thinking, and attitude. Without these three vital components, no system, method, or plan will be successful in the long run.

The first and absolutely most important step that you must take in order to be wealthy is internal, not external. Before you can be wealthy on the outside, you first must be rich of mind and heart on the inside. At the outset of this book, I mentioned that, as a financial advisor, I meet with hundreds of people every year whose financial circumstances range from modest to magnificent. One would think that those of magnificent means are always happy and satisfied without a care or worry—but that is not the case at all. I once met with an attorney and his wife whose estate was worth millions of dollars. They owned several homes with no mortgages, and had little debt. The attorney was 82 years old and his wife nearly the same. However, their reason for seeking a meeting with me was that the attorney had a strong desire to retire—remember, he was already 82!—but both he and his wife shared a nagging fear that they did not have enough money to last them the rest of their lives. They were spending in excess of $750,000 a year, but could not tell me what they spent it on. I started by helping them to assess their spending habits. Whether they were actually unable to remember what they spent their money on, or were simply too embarrassed to disclose the truth of their situation, they could only account for a little over a half-million dollars. Imagine that! Could you possibly spend $250,000 and not be able to explain where it went—and have virtually nothing to show for it? Well, it happens all the time. Considering that these two were both rapidly approaching the end of their average lifespans, having a bank account with more than $10 million in it should have been very comforting and more than enough to satisfy their needs, even lavishly. But it was not.

The point is that this couple—with far more money than 98% of the American population has at their discretion—was not rich. Despite their money, nothing could satiate their appetites and satisfy their self-image. They were poor and wanting paupers on the inside, and nothing from the outside could turn them into princes.

Conversely, I have met with many people who, with several decades of retirement in front of them, have modest means, many with less than $1 million at their disposal, and they simply cannot imagine needing more than they have. I spend time with these folks discussing how best to leave their wealth to their grandchildren or charitable concerns. They are rich inside, because they have a satisfied self-image and derive great joy from their station in life. They are princes in their own heart, and that is the most important achievement one can pursue.

Now that I have gotten up on my soapbox about attitude and self-worth, let's also admit that we do need money to survive and thrive. The point of this self-help book is to actually help you get richer, not just in a philosophical sense, but also in a tangible, monetary way. More than 50% of Americans earn less than $35,000 per year. Self-discovery is great, but we also need to take real and practical action to actually accumulate wealth and keep it, and you will do just that.

To those of you in this situation, I offer this: I want to acknowledge that many people find the prospect of fixing their financial woes daunting and depressing. Take heart! Your life can and will change in ways that are beyond imagining right now…if you do the work we have discussed. Your future is bright and happy, if you will just let it unfold for you. Regardless of your circumstances, with some luck, hard work, and time, everything can change for you.

In the way of proof, let's talk about my financial client, Al. During his working life, Al worked for a major manufacturing company as a trainer. He was comfortable and happy, and would retire well, though he would not have described himself as wealthy. The future looked comfortable for him—and then tragedy struck. At the age of 59, Al's beloved wife died. He was crushed by the loss, and became unable to work due to his overwhelming grief. In time, because of not being able to work, Al lost everything he had: his home, his savings, everything. By the time he was 62, when many people are eyeing retirement, he found himself almost penniless. During this three-year period, however, Al was able to move past his grief, and he found he was able to start working again. He went to work with a renewed focus and energy, not even thinking about his financial situation. He made money, lived simply, and saved what he could, without even counting his savings as he went.

I met Al 10 years later, when he was 72. By then he had, through hard work and focus, dramatically changed his situation. He had gone from having no home and no money to having a house that was totally paid for, no debt, and almost $1 million in savings and IRAs. He was also newly married to a wonderful woman he had met at church. When I asked Al how he had accomplished such a dramatic transformation, he said that he really was not even aware of the change as it happened. He said that he simply focused on where he was in the moment, finding joy in his work and his daily life, and letting the future take care of itself.

There are two tremendous lessons to be learned from my friend Al. The first is that we simply cannot sacrifice happiness today by being overly concerned about tomorrow. We do not know what tomorrow will bring. I have a business associate, also a financial advisor, who had a friend who spent his entire 30-year work life in a job at a company that he absolutely hated. The emotional impact was terrible: He was a mean-spirited, angry man who felt the world owed him his retirement, which he would take from the pension earned from this job he hated. Finally the day came when he could retire, which he did as expediently as possible. Unfortunately, only two years after he retired, he died of a stroke.

It was the definition of a tragedy: To have sacrificed happiness his entire life for the prospect of retirement, only to enjoy it for just two short years. The only one winner in that situation was the company, which only had to honor the pension payments for such a short time.

Much of what I have written in this volume is designed to encourage you to think differently about how you define wealth and happiness today, in the here and now. With a proper attitude and outlook, we can enjoy princely happiness—even if we are not living in the palace of our dreams. Try to manage your self-image so that you do not lose sight of daily joys.

The second lesson that Al teaches us is this: Whatever our current circumstances are, no matter how distressing or difficult, they are only temporary. We can outlast them until happiness presents itself at our door, until joy is our constant companion. Sometimes we can work hard to make that happen, and sometimes it is offered through nothing we have done at all. Circumstances change, with or without our help.

You may remember an Oscar-nominated movie called *Cast Away*, about a man named Chuck (played by Tom Hanks) who was marooned on a deserted island in the Pacific Ocean. The closing sequence to this movie is one of my favorite messages of hope. I think about it often, particularly when I have had periods of stress. After the hapless castaway has spent four years marooned on the island, a plastic portable toilet washes up onto his beach. Chuck sits, looking at this thing propped up in the sand. A breeze blows the plastic wall over and we see him come to an epiphany: He can use this piece of trash as a sail to escape the island prison, which he does.

Upon rejoining civilization, we see Chuck sitting in an office with an old workmate, talking wistfully and solemnly about his experience on the island. He talks about how demoralizing it was to be in constant near-starvation, thirsting, without basic human necessities, without shelter, without human contact. He talks about getting so low that he contemplates suicide and tries to hang himself, but is unable to because the tree limb breaks. He finally accepts that he has absolutely no control over his situation, his survival, his life, or even his death—and so he simply continues to live, day to day. Then, Chuck says, "One day, the tide brought me a sail—and everything changed."

So many Americans are in situations where their outlook seems hopeless, whether by their own hand or because the economic engine around them has ground them down. Yet, whatever our circumstances, there are many times in our lives when, through no efforts of our own, the opportunity to change everything will present itself. It happens. It happens to virtually everyone, often multiple times during our lives. The trick is to recognize it when it does happen, and to have the courage to take advantage of it.

This is why there is no formula for getting rich quick in this book. The opportunity to become wealthy within yourself is already there—and the opportunity to be wealthy on the outside will present itself many times during your life. What that opportunity looks like will be different for everyone. For some, it may present itself as an idea for an invention that you can develop, manufacture, and market. For others, it may be seeing a need for a service in your community that is not being offered—just waiting for someone bold enough to capitalize. For yet others, financial independence may come in the form of improving skills that you already have, and making yourself more valuable to your customers. Or you may have an epiphany and develop a plan to take some money or asset that you already have, investing in it wisely to see it grow over time.

As an example, I own about 2.5 acres of investment real estate near my home in Sedona that I originally purchased to resell as a house lot. The real estate market in northern Arizona has not, however, recovered sufficiently to make a sale attractive to me. However, during the past 10 years, this part of Arizona has gradually transformed itself into a vibrant wine-producing area—similar to what Sonoma, California might have looked like 20 years ago. There is high demand for viticultural land. I recently met someone in the industry and it hit me like a hammer: Why can't I plant grapes on my 2.5 acres and lease the land to a local vintner? I can plant the vines; they can cultivate and manage the harvest. Instead of making a single $60,000 sale and be done with it, I can have the land earn $10,000 a year for the next 40 years, and then pass the asset down to my daughter. My investment could pay off not three- or four-fold, but a hundred-fold!

Opportunity…it lurks around every corner.

Hope…it is the life water of your potential.

The point is this: Whatever your current circumstances, however old you are, and whatever you have to work with, your potential to become wealthy both in your heart and in your pocketbook is out there. With the right outlook on life, not only can you go out and find it, but it will beat down your door if you are open to it. You can be a prince if you educate yourself to pursue the correct goals. To do so, meditate on these lessons:

LESSON 1:

American culture—whether in the form of urban living, media, mainstream educational systems, the lure of the middle class myth, or the retirement propaganda—is designed to control your expectations, aspirations, spending habits, and attitudes about what is valuable and what is not. Rather than be a hamster on the wheel, alongside the 98% of Americans who will never get off, use it to your advantage by discovering business and investment opportunities that exploit the system.

LESSON 2:

Opportunity is abundant if you can avoid the pattern of giving back everything that you earn in pursuit of the American dream. You must decide what your dream looks like—keeping in mind that most of what you are offered out there is not for your own good, but is designed to keep you in "indentured" servitude.

LESSON 3:

No one can fix things for you but you, because only you understand what your hopes and dreams are and what you value in life. Only you can map out a way to get there that is really in your best interests. The government will not be able to keep its promises, nor will many other institutions in the future. You cannot leave your future to someone else to manage.

LESSON 4:

The secret of life, the secret of success, and the secret of happiness amount to one thing. What that one thing is, however, differs for everyone. Be careful not to let someone else dictate it to you, because it should form the foundation of your decision making and priorities. Also, your one thing should be of noble purpose to see you through the hard times—so simple pursuit of money cannot be your one thing, because money has no intrinsic value.

LESSON 5:

Visualize yourself as a prince, with your one thing in mind, and know with absolute certainty that it is yours for the taking. Don't fixate on the potential for defeat, which becomes a self-fulfilling prophecy. Surround yourself with winners. Spend your time on what you excel at and leave the rest so that you can focus on the goal. *Look through the curve.*

LESSON 6:

An asset gives, a liability takes, and almost everything in life can be classified as either giving or taking. Be fearless and thorough in your assessment of what you pursue, own, desire, even love. You will only make progress when your assets outnumber your liabilities. Since almost everything that the system recommends to you is a liability, you will need to be very critical and selective.

LESSON 7:

Do the math. It will fall to you and you alone to secure your own future and that of your family. Take advantage of every legitimate opportunity to beat the math of our country's demographics, because at the end of the day, the government will have no choice but to raise taxes and decrease benefits.

LESSON 8:

Time is the most valuable thing that you possess. It is also the great equalizer. Everyone has the same amount of time in a day, week, and year. It is also the one thing on the planet that cannot be manufactured or reproduced. Therefore, you must change your thinking about time. Choose to be industrious with your available time. There is no such thing as spare time.

LESSON 9:

No matter what your income is, find a way to start saving money. Initially, invest in safe investments; wait to roll the dice until later when you can afford to lose a little, but get started. Remember the Rule of 72 and the advantages that compounding offers. Remember, "A journey of a thousand miles begins with one step."

LESSON 10:

There are only two kinds of investments: fixed and variable. A fixed investment means your money is protected, whereas a variable investment means your money is at risk. Don't take that risk if you can't afford the loss and if you can afford some risk, make sure that your savings are actually diversified. Despite what the investing industry tells you, stocks, bonds, and mutual funds are not a diversified portfolio.

LESSON 11:

Always be on. Always be learning. There should be no distinction between work time and leisure time, and there should be no fixed definition of what you do to earn money. Reject the thinking that your brain shuts down after you put in your eight hours. It is often during the non-working hours when our greatest revelations and opportunities present themselves. Remember that Archimedes moments are usually when life-changing epiphanies happen—and they will be completely missed opportunities if your brain shuts down just because they are outside of your office hours.

LESSON 12:

Because you are the average of your five closest associates, it is your responsibility to surround yourself with people who will elevate you, not weigh you down. The right associates will help you both recognize and capitalize on opportunities to enrich your future.

Finally ...

LESSON 13:

You make your own luck. You make your own destiny. With the proper mindset, with a heart full of hope, joy, and optimistic expectations—instead of fear, pessimism and greed—your future as a prince is entirely within your grasp.

I wish you joy and success on your journey.

ABOUT THE AUTHOR

Peter M. Yachimski, RLS, is an author, an Arizona Registered Professional Land Surveyor, a practicing Construction Manager, and a licensed Financial and Income Planning specialist. He is president and managing member of several consulting firms, including Vanguard Professional Services, a real estate investment and development consulting firm; Secure Financial Solutions, a personal finance, retirement and income planning consulting firm; and Vanguard Land Investments, a real estate investment and holding company. Peter has served his clients as a professional witness and is recognized by the State of Colorado court system as an expert in real estate investments and development, and was appointed to a special task force by the office of the Governor of Arizona to review the management of state real estate assets. Peter has been providing business and personal financial guidance to clients for more than 30 years and has been a resident of Arizona for 17 years.

COMING SOON
from
PETER M. YACHIMSKI

PRINCE or PAUPER:
Prepare for the Road Ahead

In *Prepare for the Road Ahead*, Peter M. Yachimski outlines specific tools that can make a huge difference in your perspective and financial strategies. Topics include:

- How to make gains in your retirement portfolio after you start making withdrawals by using the principles of reverse dollar cost averaging.

- Why our national debt demands that you take control of your own future—and how to protect yourself when the house of cards collapses.

- Why Medicare and Medicaid are in crisis—and a unique strategy to hedge against rising taxes or falling benefits that could threaten your savings.

- Government legislation that you should be aware of so that you can protect your assets in an environment of extreme risk.

- How to use the laws governing the banking industry to your advantage in negotiating with creditors when you make a mistake.

www.ingramcontent.com/pod-product-compliance
Lightning Source LLC
Chambersburg PA
CBHW052024290426
44112CB00014B/2373